T175 NETWORKED LIVING

Exploring Information
Communication Techno

GW00493003

Block 1
Living in a networked world
Parts 1–3

Prepared on behalf of the course team
by Clem Herman and Elaine Thomas

This publication forms part of an Open University course T175 *Networked living: exploring information and communication technologies*. Details of this and other Open University courses can be obtained from the Student Registration and Enquiry Service, The Open University, PO Box 197, Milton Keynes MK7 6BJ, United Kingdom: tel. +44 (0)870 333 4340, email general-enquiries@open.ac.uk

Alternatively, you may visit the Open University website at http://www.open.ac.uk where you can learn more about the wide range of courses and packs offered at all levels by The Open University.

To purchase a selection of Open University course materials visit http://www.ouw.co.uk, or contact Open University Worldwide, Michael Young Building, Walton Hall, Milton Keynes MK7 6AA, United Kingdom for a brochure. tel. +44 (0)1908 858785; fax +44 (0)1908 858787; email ouwenq@open.ac.uk

The Open University
Walton Hall, Milton Keynes
MK7 6AA

First published 2005. Second edition 2007.

Copyright © 2005, 2007 The Open University

All rights reserved. No part of this publication may be reproduced, stored in a retrieval system, transmitted or utilised in any form or by any means, electronic, mechanical, photocopying, recording or otherwise, without written permission from the publisher or a licence from the Copyright Licensing Agency Ltd. Details of such licences (for reprographic reproduction) may be obtained from the Copyright Licensing Agency Ltd, Saffron House, 6–10 Kirby Street, London EC1N 8TS; website http://www.cla.co.uk/.

Open University course materials may also be made available in electronic formats for use by students of the University. All rights, including copyright and related rights and database rights, in electronic course materials and their contents are owned by or licensed to The Open University, or otherwise used by The Open University as permitted by applicable law.

In using electronic course materials and their contents you agree that your use will be solely for the purposes of following an Open University course of study or otherwise as licensed by The Open University or its assigns.

Except as permitted above you undertake not to copy, store in any medium (including electronic storage or use in a website), distribute, transmit or re-transmit, broadcast, modify or show in public such electronic materials in whole or in part without the prior written consent of The Open University or in accordance with the Copyright, Designs and Patents Act 1988.

Edited and designed by The Open University.

Typeset in Europe by the Alden Group, Oxford.

Printed and bound in the United Kingdom by Halstan Printing Group, Amersham.

ISBN 978 0 7492 1525 5

2.1

COURSE TEAM LIST

Karen Kear, course team chair

Ernie Taylor, course manager

Patricia Telford, course secretary

Academic staff

Mustafa Ali

Chris Bissell

David Chapman

Geoff Einon

Clem Herman

Allan Jones

Roger Jones

John Monk

Nicky Moss

Elaine Thomas

Mirabelle Walker

Judith Williams

John Woodthorpe

Media production staff

Geoff Austin

Deirdre Bethune

Annette Booz

Sophia Braybrooke

Sarah Crompton

Jamie Daniels

Vicky Eves

Alison George

Mark Kesby

Lynn Short

External assessor

Prof. Philip Witting, University of Glamorgan

Contents

Part 1
ICTs in everyday life

Clem Herman

Study Session 1: The network society

Before going any further with this study session, you should make sure that you have read through the Block 1 Companion. The Companion forms the first part of this study session so you will need to read it before continuing here.

This course is about understanding the networked world we live in. Whether we are aware of it or not, we are surrounded by networks through which information flows constantly. Our notions of time and location are changing – the world has become a global village where distance is no longer a barrier to commercial or social contact. If we live in Britain or other parts of the westernised world, it's difficult to imagine being without all the networked infrastructure that plays a crucial part in our daily lives.

In this course you'll be introduced to the underlying technologies that drive these networks and gain an understanding of how they work. You'll examine how they are applied in practice and explore some of the issues and debates that surround the introduction of these technologies in a range of everyday situations. You'll see how ICTs have enabled us to communicate and share information in ways that would have been astonishing even a few decades ago. However you'll also see how the underlying principles of information and communication technologies are based on ideas that have been around for a great deal longer, and have developed gradually, building on earlier solutions.

1.1 Data and information

Although this course is about Information and Communication Technologies, the technologies you'll be learning about do not actually handle information. Instead they handle data. In everyday language the terms 'data' and 'information' are often used interchangeably, but it is important to understand the difference when you are studying ICTs.

Data is a representation of information so that it can be conveyed, manipulated or stored. **Information** is the meaning that people give to data in particular contexts. So data can't really be considered information until it is given meaning and is interpreted.

data
information

1.2 What are ICTs?

Before you go any further, it will be useful to have a working understanding of the term 'ICT'. What exactly do we mean by 'information and communication technologies'? Your understanding

**information and
communication
technologies (ICTs)**

of this term will broaden and deepen as the course progresses, but here is a simple definition.

ICTs are the technologies used in the conveying, manipulation and storage of data by electronic means.

Let me give you some examples. In a landline telephone system, messages are conveyed as signals on wires. The message is conveyed electronically. Manipulation of data takes place when you speak into the phone – your words are transformed into electronic signals. The data is then conveyed through the phone system, stored briefly for further processing on the way, and transformed back into words at the other end. In a mobile phone system, messages are also stored and manipulated but in this case they are conveyed by electromagnetic means such as radio waves, which are wireless.

Activity 1 (exploratory)

Using the explanation of ICTs given above, would you say that the technologies used for email communication are ICTs?

Comment

When you send an email the contents are transformed into electronic signals that pass through various computer networks to reach the destination computer. The signals are then transformed back into characters on the screen.

In this example, the information is conveyed by electronic means, and it is also manipulated and stored – so email does indeed fit our definition of an ICT.

In T175 we are going to be studying not just the technologies used to convey, manipulate and store data but also the systems that are used in this conveying, manipulation and storage. Examples of ICT systems include the internet, mobile phone systems, broadcast radio and TV systems, but ICTs are also essential to many other day-to-day activities. Consider for example a visit to a supermarket. Checkout personnel use an ICT system to scan bar codes and obtain prices. ICT systems also allow management to monitor stock levels and sales trends. In fact, you'll be looking at exactly such a system in Part 2 of this block.

1.3   Technology and society

ICT systems are increasingly embedded in many aspects of our daily lives. But ICTs don't just exist in a vacuum; they have an impact on society, and society has an effect on them. They also have economic and political implications. These aspects of ICT systems are also introduced and discussed in T175.

The end of the twentieth century and the beginning of the twenty-first century are often compared to other historical periods of great technological change such as the Industrial Revolution. This is because of the huge changes that are happening in many aspects of life. The terms **information society** and **network society** have been used to analyse the social and economic changes that are taking place in conjunction with technological developments. These ideas are used by policy makers to drive forward changes in our technological infrastructure. For example the UK government's vision is that many public services will be accessible online, and billions of pounds have been spent to get computers into schools and local communities. The language used by politicians has drawn strongly on the inevitability of technological change and the need to be at the forefront of these changes in order to secure future prosperity.

One of the discussions about ICTs concerns whether changes in society are driven by technological development, or whether technologies are actually influenced and shaped by the society that produces them. This is a complex debate but an interesting idea to think about. On the one hand, if technologies are shaped by social conditions, then they will inevitably reflect the values and norms of the particular society in which they are created. On the other hand, if we believe technology determines the way society develops, then we might feel very helpless and fatalistic. You could also think about this on a personal level. In your everyday life, you will probably have experienced technological change as something that you have no control over – something that happens to you. For example, a new computer arrives in your office and you are required to learn how to use it, whether you like it or not. Often you have no influence or control over how technology intrudes into your life. In commercial terms this is sometimes described as either a 'technology push' or, conversely, a 'market pull'.

Yet technologies are also shaped by the people who design and create them. Societies and individuals can also control or influence how technologies are used. New mobile phones with added features seem to appear every month and relentless advertising tries to persuade us that we need to have the latest version. However, as the consumer you do have ultimate control over whether you choose to buy one or not.

Unintended uses sometimes develop for technologies. A classic example is the SMS/text messaging facility on mobile phones. Originally, this was just a minor feature and was not expected by the manufacturers to be used by phone owners at all – yet it resulted in a whole new method of communication and form of popular culture, different ways of interacting with radio and television and even a new language form (texting). ICTs also have to be seen in a political context – those with power (often governments) can influence how technologies are taken up, for example by funding the development of broadband network infrastructure or indeed by restricting this growth.

information
society

network society

Our views about technology are influenced by many factors, often by what is presented in the media (Figure 1).

Figure 1 Scene from *The Day The Earth Stood Still*

Think about how people viewed technology in the past. In the 1960s, the cartoon series *The Jetsons* had a mechanical maid called Rosie the Robot. Images of the future at this time often included robots, androids or machines that looked like humans, some of which have materialised while others remain in the realms of science fiction. Forty years later, domestic technologies such as dishwashers, microwaves and washing machines have become taken for granted in most UK households, but they are very different from the humanoid robots some people imagined.

Activity 2 (exploratory)

In the following extract, which was written in 2004, Ian Pearson, BT's 'futurologist', makes a prediction about everyday life in 2010.

Read the article keeping in mind the following questions: How accurately do you think it predicts the future? Have any of his predictions come true yet?

THE FUTURE OF EVERYDAY LIFE IN 2010

Ian Pearson, 2004

[...]

By 2010, some of today's industries will be dead, mostly those with 'agent' in the title, replaced by computer programmes running for free. Many tasks in every job will be automated in much the same way. Computers will become intelligent personal assistants, greatly boosting our productivity. Most things that we thought need human creativity can even be automated. Computers already write good music for instance. What will be left are those areas of work that need the human touch. We will quickly move through the information economy into the care economy, exploring what it is we want from each other when we can automate most of the physical and mental bits of our work.

[...]

Equipment for the roaming worker will have access to the network via satellite or terrestrial systems. People will control computers and services simply by talking in everyday language. Computers will understand all major languages and understand what the user means most of the time, asking clarification questions to resolve any ambiguities or omissions. They will be able to read out documents or messages after sorting out what is important from the junk. Where appropriate, images can be displayed on imaginary screens floating in space. Users would simply wear lightweight glasses with projectors built into each arm and semi-reflective lens to give full 3 dimensional pictures. Active contact lenses that use laser beams drawing pictures straight onto the wearer's retinas would be in late stages of development by 2010. We could expect to have robocop style information in our field of view, overlaid on the real world. Finding somewhere will mean following the arrow floating in front of you. Satellite positioning and navigation will do all the hard work. Later still, we will see video relayed to computers that recognise people in our field of view, telling us who they are and a little about them if we want. The embarrassment of forgetting someone's name or where you met them will be history.

[...]

Network based life will affect home too. A selection of screens hanging on walls may display works of art, static or moving. Or they may act as virtual fish tanks, or virtual windows looking out onto a Bahamas beach. Or you may have a cup of coffee with a distant friend, with life sized video images. The coffee may well be made and brought to you by a robot, even by 2010. Other insect-like robots might be keeping the carpets clean, trimming the grass, tidying up, or monitoring household security. But the most widespread use of robotics in the home by 2010 will be as pets. We may have cute, cuddly robots that look like kittens, teddy bears or R2D2 according to taste. They will wander around doing cute things, respond to their names, do tricks, speak and make appropriate facial expressions. They will understand simple

instructions and conversation. Best of all, they may have a radio link to a smart computer elsewhere in the house that will give them even more functionality remotely. So the pet itself may be little more than a walking robot with video cameras for eyes, microphones for ears and a speaker in its mouth. But with this radio link it will be able to act as an interface to the global superhighway and all that it holds. You could tell the pet what you want to do and it will arrange it, or rather its big brother under the stairs will arrange it.

[...]

Comment

How accurately do you think it predicts the future?

It seems to me that the author is making quite sweeping statements aimed at portraying a utopian vision of the future. The second paragraph shown here seems quite feasible, although voice recognition software hasn't improved as quickly as people expected. Some of the ideas seem to come straight from science fiction films, but this might be because that is what other people think the future will be like.

Have any of his predictions come true yet?

Robotic pets are already available, but not very widely adopted. And there are already wearable devices such as glasses with built-in video screens.

Predicting the future is always a difficult business and we should not take this too seriously. However most technological change does not happen overnight. As you study this course, you will develop your understanding of the basic principles and processes involved in ICT systems. This will put you in a better position to distinguish between fact and science fiction.

Study Session 2: Your networked life

The next activity aims to get you thinking a bit more about how ICT systems form part of your own life and to make you more aware of how you are living in a networked world. ICT systems are embedded in many everyday experiences and we have become so used to this that we hardly notice that we are using them.

Activity 3 (exploratory)

Think about a typical day and list the different ways in which you communicate, or are communicated with, using technology. What communication devices (pieces of equipment) or networked systems can you think of that are involved?

For example when you send an email from home the communication devices and systems would include your computer, plus your telephone or cable line, plus the internet.

Write your answers in a table format, as shown in the following example (Table 1).

Table 1

Examples of communication using technology	Devices or systems used
sending an email from home	computer, telephone/cable line, internet

Comment

Table 2 contains some examples of the kinds of things I came up with and the sort of detail I was able to give about the devices and systems. I expect your list will be a bit different. Notice how important networks are in all of my examples. Was the same true for yours?

Table 2

Examples of communication using technology	Devices or systems used
Reading train information at a station	Electronic noticeboard to display information. Some sort of networked information system in the station – all the noticeboards are updated at the same time.
Getting into my office building	Bar code on swipe card, card reader at the door. Network to central computer to verify that I am authorised to enter.
Emailing a colleague from my work computer	My computer. Network linking my computer to my colleague's computer.
Making a phone call from a landline telephone	Handset and telephone line to local exchange. Network of telephone exchanges.
Sending a text message on my mobile phone	Mobile phone. Wireless connection into mobile phone network.
Playing a computer game with others online from my home computer.	Personal computer, telephone line and modem or other network connection. The internet that links my computer to other players' computers.
Finding out my bank balance from an ATM machine	Bank card and PIN, ATM machine. Bank network linking ATMs and central computers holding customer data.
Watching TV	TV set, remote control (to switch on and change channels), aerial (or antenna) or cable link to receive signals from the TV broadcasters. Broadcasting network that transmits signals from TV station.

2.1   ICT systems in everyday life

In Activity 3 you identified some of the ICT systems and devices that you use for communication, which are part of your immediate environment. These devices do not operate in isolation but need to be part of an information and communication system – linked to other devices with the capability to transfer data between them. All the examples above are therefore associated with networks of one kind or another.

During the rest of the course you will be studying in more detail how ICT networks and systems work. Here are some examples of situations where ICTs are having an impact on our everyday lives.

2.1.1　Finance

Every time you use a debit or credit card the shop till uses a terminal connected to other computers via a network. Your identification details are automatically transferred from your card to your bank or credit card company for verification and your balance adjusted accordingly. This also applies if you are shopping online, or over the phone (when booking a cinema ticket, for example). ATMs (also known as cashpoints) allow you to check your bank balance or withdraw cash from wherever you are in the world. The machines are networked to a central computer, which has records of your account in a filing system known as a **database**. Many banks also provide banking services via the internet, minimising the need for customers to visit a branch.

database

Financial services have undergone huge changes in recent years as a result of the development of ICT systems. This has led to the need for increased security procedures to combat new types of fraud. It has also led to changes in many areas of commerce; for example, the role of travel agents has changed as more people book their own holidays directly online.

Some types of business have disappeared completely as online and computer-based information have taken their place. For example, you rarely see door-to-door insurance salesmen these days! Similarly, new types of business have been created, such as online auctions like eBay. Existing business types have been transformed through the use of ICT systems, for example the development of online booksellers such as Amazon.

2.1.2　The internet

As well as impacting on the commercial world, the internet has had an enormous impact on all areas of life. While there are still people in many parts of the world who do not have access to an internet connection, the majority of people in the developed world now have access either at home or at work, and have the opportunity to use online information resources, or communicate with others using email, instant messaging or discussion groups. New online communities have developed and existing communities have created new ways of communicating. However, issues of identity and security have become a concern. New technologies have engendered new types of crime, including identity theft and financial frauds. These problems have fostered the development of new security technologies.

The internet has become a major factor in enabling information sharing and has had a huge impact on the availability of information of all kinds. Material on the internet reflects widely differing viewpoints and sources: from official news bulletins to unofficial rumours, and from

commercial megastores to community portals. The internet has revolutionised the way information can be published, raising questions about the authority and regulation of content. Because of the way the internet has been designed, no individual government, company or person has control over it.

2.1.3 Entertainment

The world of entertainment is constantly evolving with the advent of new technologies. Digital broadcasting has changed the way we experience television, with more interactive programming and participation. Digital cameras, printers and scanners have enabled more people to experiment with image production. Computer gaming has been an important influence in the development of graphical interfaces. Technology has been at the forefront of changes in the production and distribution of music, as well as in the ways in which people can access and listen to music.

2.1.4 Public services

In the UK, in many NHS trusts, patient records are easily shared between departments within a hospital. These electronic patient records may soon be transferable across the whole health service, so that medical staff can access them from any part of the NHS. In some places, especially remote rural areas, doctors may be able to make use of computer networks to make a diagnosis if they are unable to see the patient in person.

Passenger information is increasingly available via networked computers: for example train timetables, information in stations and airports, real-time information over the internet. Networked communication systems are also crucial in the control of transport systems, from traffic lights and pedestrian crossings to air traffic control and train signals.

Many government services in the UK are now available online. For example you can renew or apply for a passport, book a driving test, claim benefits, fill in your tax returns – you can even report suspect activity to MI5! Local authorities provide information services online, and there are numerous opportunities to learn online as you are doing now with The Open University.

2.2 ICTs and you

Sometimes it's useful to stop and think a bit about your own experiences and focus on your own views. This can help you understand issues in more depth. For example when studying the impact of ICTs on everyday life, your own experiences are a useful resource.

Activity 4 (exploratory)

Think of ways in which your own life has changed as a result of the introduction of ICTs. This could be at work, in your education, in your leisure-time activities, or in your own home. Are all of these changes things that you have welcomed? Or are there areas where you would have preferred things to stay the same?

Comment

I'm aware of how different things are for my children. For example when they are doing homework they will regularly search for information on the internet, rather than using textbooks as I did when I was at school. It means they can get what they need quickly although I am sometimes concerned that what they find may not be the most accurate or authoritative source on a topic.

For myself the internet has been very beneficial. I am able to work from home using my PC and internet connection, which means I can cut down on travelling time because I don't have to be in the office every day. But I have to watch my work–life balance, as my alternative 'office' is always open!

So far in this session you've been looking at the ICT systems that are part of your everyday life, including those in your own home. One of the difficulties that can emerge with the development of so many new technologies is the issue of coordinating and controlling all these systems. One solution to this is a concept called the 'smart home'.

2.3 ICT systems at home

Most homes in the UK contain a variety of systems for entertainment, lighting, security, heating and so on. The idea of a **smart home** is to integrate the control of these systems. So, for example, if you are away from home and want to make sure the house is warm for when you get back, you could call the house and switch the central heating on.

smart home

At this point we aren't going to go into any more detail about how the smart home works, but the following activity uses some of the data from a survey about smart homes for you to develop your skills in interpreting data. In later blocks you'll be developing your own diagrams and graphs using data from course materials; but for now we will simply look at how a survey like this can be interpreted.

Activity 5 (self-assessment)

Using the graph in Figure 2, answer the following questions:

(a) What percentage of people thought that being able to control devices in the home when they were out, would be useful to them?

(b) What percentage didn't think safety or security were important?

(c) Did more people like or dislike the idea of one remote control to control everything in the home? Why do you think people might not like this idea?

(d) If you were responsible for marketing smart homes, which of these factors (control, safety/security, single remote) do you think you would be emphasising?

(e) Would you like to live in a smart home? Why? Or why not?

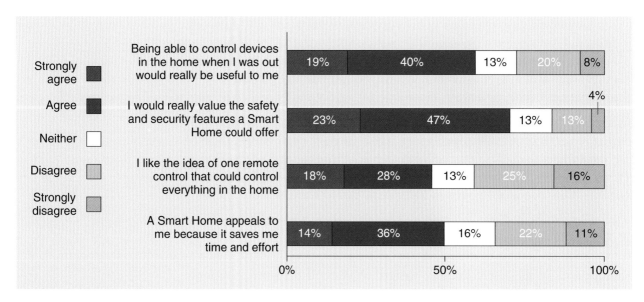

Figure 2   Results of a survey on smart home features (source: Pragnell, November 2000) [Note that the bottom entry does not total 100%]

Comment

My answers are given at the end of this part.

If you want to find out more details about this smart home project you can visit **http://www.jrf.org.uk/housingandcare/smarthomes/**

The remainder of Block 1 Part 1 will require you to be at your computer and have access to the internet. You should now go to the T175 website and follow the links for Block 1, Part 1, Study Sessions 3 and 4.

ANSWERS TO SELF-ASSESSMENT ACTIVITIES

Activity 5

(a) 59% – I included those who strongly agreed as well as those who agreed with the first statement (19% plus 40%).

(b) 17% – I included those who strongly disagreed and those who disagreed with the second statement (4% plus 13%).

(c) 46% liked the idea of one remote control, while 41% disliked the idea – so there was not a lot of difference. Perhaps some people were worried that it would be easy to lose or that as a single control it would be too complex and therefore difficult to operate.

(d) I'd probably be emphasising safety and security as 70% of the respondents thought these were important factors.

(e) I'd like the convenience but I'd have to be sure that everything was going to work. I think I'd be a bit concerned about the house taking over control of my life!

REFERENCES

Pearson, I. (2004) *The Future of Everyday Life in 2010*, British Telecommunications plc. [online] http://www.bt.com/sphere/insights/pearson/everyday.htm [Accessed 3 March 2005]

Pragnell, M., Spence, L., and Moore R. (November, 2000) *The Market Potential for Smart Homes*, N40, Joseph Rowntree Foundation [online], York Publishing Services http://www.jrf.org.uk/knowledge/findings/housing/n40.asp [Accessed 3 March 2005]

ACKNOWLEDGEMENTS

Grateful acknowledgement is made to the following sources for permission to reproduce material within this product.

Text

Pearson, I. (2004) 'The Future of Everyday Life in 2010', British Telecommunications plc.

Figures

Figure 1: Ronald Grant Archive

Figure 2: From the *Findings The market potential for Smart Homes* published in 2000 by the Joseph Rowntree Foundation. Reproduced by permission of the Joseph Rowntree Foundation.

Part 2
Introducing ICT systems

Elaine Thomas

Study Session 1: Describing an ICT system

In Part 2 I shall be introducing you to some ideas about how ICT systems work. Because this part of Block 1 is about ICT *systems*, I'll be starting with a discussion about what constitutes a system. I'll go on to introduce some diagrammatic ways of representing ICT systems. Then I'll look at some examples to illustrate how they carry out the processes you read about in Part 1, namely conveying, storing and manipulating data. You will also find out about other processes performed by ICT systems.

In this study session I'll start by discussing how taking a 'systems' view of ICT systems can help our understanding of them. Later in the session, I'll be focusing on the communication component of an ICT system.

1.1   Exploring systems

There are many types of **system** – not just ICT systems. For example, we all have a nervous system and, as you are studying T175, you are in a higher education system. Our homes have plumbing systems and electrical systems.

system

Activity 1 (exploratory)

What systems do you come across in your daily life? Write down two or three examples under each of the two headings below:

Systems in your home   **Systems outside the home**

Comment

Your examples of systems might be very different from mine, but here's my list:

- In my home there are systems such as the stereo system, my (not very efficient) personal filing system, the central heating system.
- Systems outside the home include: an appointments system to see the doctor, a library system for borrowing books and other media, a booking system for a concert or the theatre.

  In the workplace there are systems such as the telephone system, the payroll system, the budgeting system, the internal mail system and, of course, the computer systems.

As you can see from my list, and probably from your own, the word 'system' can be used in a number of ways. At first glance, there may not be much in common between a nervous system and an education system or an ICT system, but they are all called 'systems' so it is likely that they share some features. One important aspect of a system is connectedness. A plumbing system, for example, involves components such as pipes, taps and valves, which are all physically connected in some way. The **components** are put together to perform a certain function, in this case to supply water to a building.

components

Systems do not always involve physical things; the components may be activities or even ideas. Putting on a concert, for example, involves activities such as hiring a hall, holding rehearsals and selling tickets. These activities can be viewed as a system for putting on a concert because they are put together in order to carry out that function.

1.1.1   A system map

system map

One way of explaining and analysing a system is to represent it in a graphical form, known as a **system map**. I'll use the example of a system for making an appointment with a doctor in a health centre to illustrate this point. In this example, the health centre uses a computerised booking system and the patient may phone or visit the health centre to make an appointment. Therefore, the system includes a patient, a receptionist, a doctor, and a computerised booking system. The example shown in Figure 1 shows how this system could be represented using a system map. I have called the system a 'health centre appointments system' and you can see a number of blobs called 'patient', 'doctor', 'receptionist', and 'computerised booking system'. These are the components of the appointments system.

system boundary

The thick line around these is the **system boundary** that defines which components are part of the system and which are outside it.

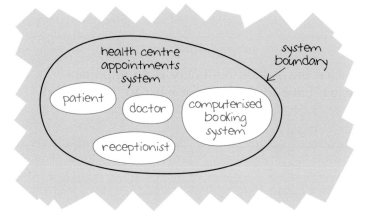

Figure 1   System map of a health centre appointments system

Subsystems

An important aspect of systems is that each component can be considered as a **subsystem**. In the health centre appointments system, the 'computerised booking system' may be a complex system in its own right involving a number of computers networked together. Figure 2 shows this view of the system with 'computerised booking system' composed of two subsystems: 'network' and 'computers'. Of course, these subsystems may also be complex systems in their own right, composed of further subsystems.

subsystem

A complex overall system can therefore be reduced to more manageable proportions by grouping components together and thinking about it in terms of subsystems. You can think of the subsystems as being 'nested' inside a system or another subsystem, a bit like Russian dolls. No single one of them is 'the doll'; each one fits inside the larger one. A system map can help by allowing us to focus on the particular systems and subsystems that we are interested in.

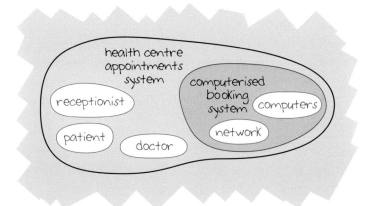

Figure 2 System map of a health centre appointments system, showing subsystems

Drawing the boundary

Deciding where to place the system boundary is an important consideration in that we have to think about what to include and exclude. This isn't always an easy decision to make and it often depends on the perspective of the person viewing the system.

The system maps in Figures 1 and 2 show the 'doctor', 'patient', 'receptionist' and 'computerised booking system' as part of the system. However, in Figure 3 the doctor and the patient are placed outside the system in an area that is called the system's **environment**; Figure 3 shows a perspective where the doctor and patient are not part of the system directly, although they influence it or are influenced by it. By placing them outside the system boundary, the focus is shifted towards the computerised booking system and how the receptionist uses it.

environment

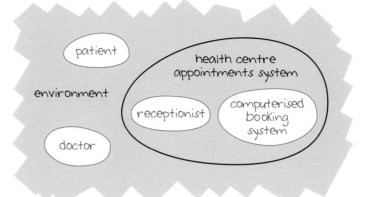

Figure 3   System map of a health centre appointments system, showing doctor and patient as part of the environment

Figure 4 illustrates yet another view of the health centre appointments system. Here the doctor and patient are seen as irrelevant and so do not appear at all in the system map. This view of an appointments system embodies yet another shift in emphasis. It is a view that might be taken by engineers who are concerned with the hardware and software of a computerised system (these are discussed in more detail in Study Session 2). However, this view is too narrow, and therefore risky, when designing new systems or planning enhancements to existing ones. Ignoring some of the users of the system or 'stakeholders' could lead to a booking system that doesn't do the job it was intended to do.

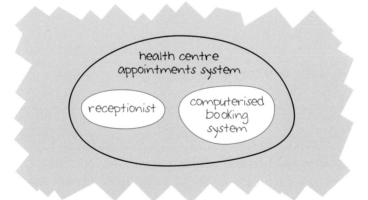

Figure 4   System map of a health centre appointments system, excluding doctor and patient

Activity 2 (exploratory)

An email communication system includes:

- the sender
- the recipient
- the sender's computer
- the recipient's computer
- the internet

Draw a system map to represent this email communication system (roughly oval outlines will be fine). Do you think the users (the sender and the recipient) should be inside the system boundary or outside it?

Comment

Figure 5 shows my system map. Where have you drawn the boundary? Does it include the sender and the recipient as the users of the system within the system boundary, or outside it? As you can see, I have drawn the users outside the system boundary, in the environment. Whether users of an email system feel outside or inside the system is an interesting question.

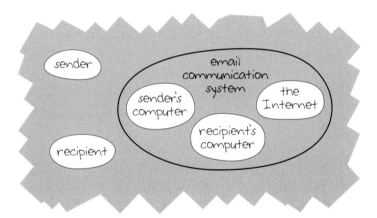

Figure 5   A system map of an email communication system

I've introduced system maps for two main reasons. Firstly, it is important to realise that systems are composed of subsystems and that these subsystems are often themselves composed of subsystems. This idea will help us as we explore ICT systems. Secondly, we may draw the system boundary in different places at different times. For example, if we want to discuss the social or economic impact of a particular ICT system, we will be drawing the boundary very widely indeed but if we want to look at how some subsystem in an ICT system works, then we will be drawing the boundary very tightly around the subsystem.

1.1.2 Models of ICT systems

To help me to introduce you to important ideas about ICT systems, I'm going to take a three-stage approach. If you think back to our working definition of ICTs in Part 1, you'll remember that ICTs involve conveying, manipulating and storing data. This is going to be the basis of my approach.

Firstly, in the remainder of this study session, we'll look at ICT systems where the primary function is to *convey* data. We can think of these systems as **communication systems** and I'll use a mobile phone system as an example.

In Study Session 2, I'll focus on ICT systems where the chief function is to *manipulate* and *store* data. A computer is a primary example of this kind of ICT system, so I'll use a personal computer like the one you are using in your study of this course as an illustration.

Finally, in Study Session 3 I'll show how the conveying, manipulating and storing of data can all come together in an ICT system. This convergence of conveying, storing and manipulating data has led to many new and exciting developments, as you will see during your study of this course.

1.2 Communication systems

Generally, when we talk about communication between humans, we mean one person conveying information to another person. Figure 6 shows a basic model, or representation, of a communication system for getting a message from the sender to the recipient. The diagram shows the sender (User 1), the message, a 'means of conveying a message' and the recipient (User 2).

block diagram

Figure 6 is an example of a **block diagram**, which is another graphical way of representing a system. Each block represents something in the real world, and the labels on the blocks tell you what that 'something' is. In this diagram I have chosen to represent people and inanimate objects in different ways. The oval shapes (which are still called 'blocks') represent the users of the communication system. The rectangular blocks represent inanimate objects in the communication system. The lines between the blocks represent the flow of something: here it is the message.

communication system

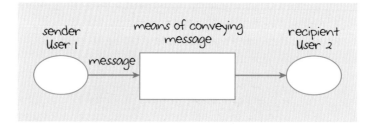

Figure 6 A basic model of a communication system

Activity 3 (exploratory)

Suppose you were planning a birthday party for someone. How could you communicate the message – that is, the details of the date, the time and the venue – to your prospective guests? Jot down four methods of communication. In each case, think of what is needed to convey the message.

Comment

The four methods of communication I thought of are as follows. If my guests live in the same house as me, or if I happened to meet the people concerned, I could just tell them the date, time and venue. If not, I could send them an invitation using the postal system. Alternatively, I could telephone them to give them the details, which involves using the telephone network. I could also email the people I wanted to invite, if I knew their email addresses, which would involve using a computer network – probably the internet.

In each of these situations we could say that communication involved a sender, a recipient, some form of message and some means of conveying the message. The various means of conveying the message in my answer include voice communication, the postal system, the telephone network and a computer network.

Activity 4 (self-assessment)

Think back to the working definition of ICTs in Part 1 of this block. Which of these four means of conveying the message involve ICTs?

Comment

The answer is given at the end of this part.

1.2.1 Looking into the 'means of conveying a message'

The diagram in Figure 6 shows that, for communication to take place, there needs to be some means of conveying the message between the sender and the recipient. I am now going to look at the essential components of 'means of conveying a message'. In other words, I shall treat 'means of conveying a message' as a system and look at its components.

Three essential components of 'means of conveying a message are: a **transmitter**, a **network** and a **receiver**. Figure 7 shows these components in a block diagram. In a mobile phone system, for example, the 'transmitter' would be User 1's mobile phone, the 'network' would be the mobile telephone network and the 'receiver' would be User 2's mobile phone.

transmitter

network

receiver

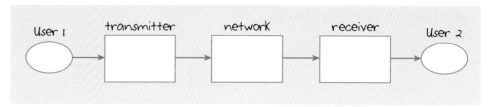

Figure 7 A more detailed model of a communication system

System components

I'll now look at what these components do in the communication system, using the mobile phone system as an example.

The transmitter

The transmitter receives a message from User 1 and manipulates it into data which can be sent into the network. The transmitter may also store or retrieve data relating to the message.

In the mobile phone system, the transmitter, which is User 1's mobile phone, receives a message from User 1 in the form of sound. It manipulates the incoming sound into a data format suitable for sending into the mobile phone network. Even basic models of mobile phone handsets can store names and telephone numbers, so in this example the transmitter is also storing and retrieving data.

The network

communication
channel

The network is a **communication channel** in that it conveys data from the transmitter to the receiver. The network may also manipulate data in some way, and it may also store or retrieve data.

In a mobile phone system, the network conveys the message from User 1's handset to User 2's. It will also store the identity of User 1 and the duration of the call. This data is used to work out the amount to charge User 1, which is a form of manipulation of data. A network can be very complex, so a call does not usually go directly from one caller to another in a single step. The network, therefore, will select the route for conveying a call through the network from the transmitter to the receiver.

The receiver

The receiver receives data from the network and manipulates it into a message to send to User 2. Sometimes the receiver may also store or retrieve data.

In the mobile phone communication system, the data received from the network must be manipulated back into sound before being sent to the user. In addition, some mobile phones can store and retrieve data about the user's contacts, so that when a call is received they can translate the phone number of the caller into a name which is then displayed.

The processes

My description of the three subsystems of 'means of conveying a message' has indicated some important processes that each carries out. These are shown in Figure 8. The key processes are those that will always be carried out and they are shown in bold; the other processes may or may not be performed. (I have used this scheme of bold text for essential processes in all block diagrams.)

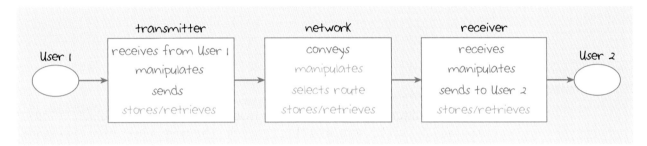

Figure 8 A model of a communication system showing the processes involved

Activity 5 (exploratory)

1 Look at the processes listed for the transmitter in Figure 8.
2 Now reread my two paragraphs about the transmitter. Underline the processes carried out by the transmitter.
3 Repeat (1) and (2) for both the network and the receiver.

Comment

Here is my paragraph about the transmitter, amended with the processes underlined.

'The transmitter <u>receives</u> a message from User 1 and <u>manipulates</u> it into data which can be <u>sent</u> into the network. The transmitter may also <u>store</u> or <u>retrieve</u> data relating to the message.

'In the mobile phone system, the transmitter, which is User 1's mobile phone, <u>receives</u> a message from User 1 in the form of sound. It <u>manipulates</u> the incoming sound into a data format suitable for <u>sending</u> into the mobile phone network. Even basic models of mobile phone handsets can <u>store</u> names and telephone numbers, so in this example the transmitter is also <u>storing</u> and <u>retrieving</u> data.'

I'll leave you to underline the processes for network and receiver yourself.

Communication links

Next I'll be looking more closely at the 'network' block in Figure 8, and in particular at the links that must be present before communication can take place. I'll introduce you to just a few of the forms that these links

can take; links may be physical ones, such as cables, or they may be wireless, such as radio links. I'll also discuss how we measure the capacity of a link for carrying messages.

cables

Physical **cables** can provide a path for conveying data between two points. A common example is the telephone wires that are used to connect the 'landline' telephones in people's homes to the nearest telephone exchange. Cables are also used to carry television and often radio signals to the homes of cable TV subscribers. Fibre-optic cables are used to interconnect telephone exchanges. Cables are also used to connect computers together into various kinds of network.

wireless

There are two forms of **wireless** link in common use: radio links and infrared. Millions of people around the world now use mobile phones, and this involves radio links. You may also have come across 'Bluetooth' and 'WiFi' radio links in connection with computers. Bluetooth® is used for short-range wireless links between devices, for example to connect a computer and a printer. A WiFi link, with its slightly longer range, might be used to connect a WiFi-enabled notebook computer to a WiFi 'hotspot' (in a café or other public place), which provides a link to the internet.

The other sort of link is an infrared link, which you will have come across when using the remote control for your television set. Infrared can also provide a communications link between computers and devices such as printers. An important difference between wireless links and infrared is that an infrared link must be along a line of sight (for example, the remote control has to be pointed at the television), whereas a radio link need not be.

capacity

It is very important that a communication link has the **capacity** to cope with the messages it has to convey – that is, that it can convey the messages as quickly as they are arriving from the transmitter. The ability of a communication link to convey data is measured by a quantity known as its 'bandwidth'. But what is bandwidth? To answer that question I need to introduce you to the form in which data is normally conveyed in today's ICT systems. This form is a series of pulses – that is, data is conveyed by sending streams of pulses from one end of a communication link to another.

Working with bits

bit

You may have met the term **bit**, perhaps in connection with computers. The term 'bit' is also important in communication systems. It is an abbreviation for 'binary digit'. A binary digit can have just one of two values: it can be either 1 or 0. Pulses can be represented by 1s and 0s, that is, as bits, and so it is convenient to think of streams of 1s and 0s being conveyed along the communications link.

data rate

bit rate

The rate at which the 1s and 0s are conveyed is known as the **data rate** or **bit rate**. Every communication link has a maximum data rate it can

bandwidth

support, and that's what we mean by the link's **bandwidth**. (You may possibly have met another meaning of the term 'bandwidth': a frequency range. That meaning is different from the one we are discussing here.) Data rate and bandwidth are both measured as a number of *bits per second*. For convenience, 'bits per second' is often abbreviated to bps. For instance the data rate might be 100 000 bps (i.e. 100 000 bits per second), 250 000 000 bps or much more.

Clearly we are going to have to deal with large numbers when talking about data rates, so I'm going to introduce a way of making these large numbers more manageable.

You will be familiar with the prefix 'kilo' in words such as kilogram, which is 1000 grams, or kilometre, which is 1000 metres. So it will come as no surprise that 1000 bits per second can also be described as a kilobit per second. The prefix 'mega' is similarly used for a million, so 1 000 000 bits per second is a megabit per second The prefix 'giga' is used for a billion (that is, a thousand million).

Activity 6 (self-assessment)

. . . .

How many bits per second are there in a gigabit per second? Write your answer in both words and figures.

Comment

The answer is given at the end of this part.

All of these prefixes have standard abbreviations. For instance, instead of writing 'kilobits per second' we can write kbps – that is, we write k for kilo. Similarly, M is used for 'mega' and G for 'giga'. (Notice that by convention the k is lower-case but the M and G are upper-case.) Table 1 summarises all this information.

Table 1   Prefixes for data rates

Prefix	In figures this is:	In words this is:	Symbol
kilo	1000	A thousand	k
mega	1 000 000	A million	M
giga	1 000 000 000	A billion (thousand million)	G

You may have come across examples of data rates and bandwidths in connection with modems and broadband. At the time of writing (early 2005) a dialup modem typically provides a data rate of 56 kbps, which is 56 000 bps, and Internet Service Providers (ISPs) advertise broadband connections with bandwidths such as 1 megabit per second (which is 1 Mbps or 1 000 000 bps).

Activity 7 (self-assessment)

Have a go at answering these questions to test your understanding of what you have read so far about communication systems.

(a) The maximum data rate that a communication link can support is called its _____.

(b) The sort of communication link used by Bluetooth is a _____ link.

(c) A WiFi link between a notebook computer and a 'hotspot' can handle data at up to 54 megabits per second (54 Mbps). How many bits per second is that?

Comment

The answers are given at the end of this part.

1.3   Conclusion

We have arrived at a model of a communication system that illustrates the processes needed for communication. We have also looked at the different kinds of communication link that can be used to convey data, and how to express the rates at which they can convey data. In the next study session, we shall be looking at a computer system as an example of an ICT system where data manipulation and storage are the most important features.

Study Session 2: Computers

In this study session, I am going to start by considering a **stand-alone computer**, which is a computer that is not connected to a network. In this type of ICT system, the key processes are the manipulation and storage of data. I'll be introducing some details about the way that a computer manipulates and stores data. Later in the study session I'll be discussing the processes that are carried out by computers when they are linked.

stand-alone computer

2.1 A stand-alone computer

The computer you are using for your studies is called a **personal computer** or PC. Although you have an internet connection for use in this course, your computer can probably also be used as a stand-alone computer. Your PC may be a **desktop computer** or a **notebook computer** (sometimes known as a **laptop computer**). Usually a desktop computer comes with separate devices such as a monitor, a keyboard, a mouse and speakers and it runs on mains electricity. Notebook computers are designed to be small and light in order to make them portable, so the screen and keyboard are part of the one unit. Notebook computers have the same capabilities as a desktop computer, but can be run on an internal battery as well as from an electrical socket. Figure 9 illustrates some types of computer.

types of computer

personal

desktop

notebook

laptop

Figure 9 Desktop and notebook/laptop computer

For a PC to manipulate data there need to be processes by which the computer receives data from the user and sends data back to the user. Hence, the block diagram in Figure 10 shows the first process associated with a stand-alone computer as 'receives from user' and the second as 'sends to user'. You will see that 'manipulates' and 'stores/retrieves' are also listed in the diagram. I'm not going to go into a lot of detail about

the inner workings of a computer here, but it will be useful for you to know something about how a computer carries out these processes. My starting point will be the 'receives from user' and 'sends to user' processes. Then I'll introduce you to the way a computer carries out its main processes: manipulation and storage.

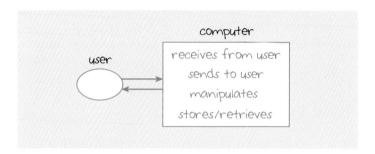

Figure 10 A model of a stand-alone computer

2.1.1 Sending and receiving data

input devices

A computer receives data from a user by means of **input devices**. The two most commonly used input devices are the keyboard and the mouse. A computer sends data to a user by means of **output devices**. Data may be output via devices such as a screen or a printer.

output devices

There are many different ways of getting data into a computer. For example, a scanner converts images and texts into a format that can be processed by the computer and displayed on screen. Devices such as touch screens and graphics tablets convert the pressure from stylus or finger strokes into data. Data from digital cameras and camcorders can also be received by a computer.

Some devices can be used for a number of purposes; for example a printer, scanner and photocopier can be combined as one physical device.

Ports

ports

On the outside of a computer you will see a number of connection points that look like sockets. These sockets are known as **ports** and they provide connections between the computer and external devices such as a digital camera or printer. Ports control the flow of data between the computer and these devices, ensuring that data is sent and received quickly and reliably.

Modern ICT devices require increasingly large amounts of data to be sent between the computer and the devices. Therefore, it is important that the ports provide a high-speed connection. Two high-speed ports currently available are Firewire and Universal Serial Bus (USB). Firewire can provide a fast connection at a rate of up to 800 megabits per second (Mbps). USB ports come in two versions: USB 1.1 and the more recent USB 2.0. The latter is faster, at about 480 Mbps, while USB 1.1 is only 12 Mbps.

You may also find older types of ports on your computer, such as a serial port, which was often used for a modem, and a parallel port, used to connect the computer to a printer.

Activity 8 (self-assessment)

(a) Which of these devices provide a means by which a computer can receive data from a user: keyboard, scanner, printer, monitor, mouse?

(b) Which type of port provides a faster connection between a computer and an input or output device: Firewire or USB?

Comment

The answes are given at the back of this part.

2.1.2   Manipulating data

A computer needs two main components to manipulate data: a processor and a working memory.

The processor

The **processor** can be thought of as the 'brain' of the computer in that it manages everything the computer does. A processor is contained on a single **microchip** or 'chip'. A **chip** is a small, thin slice of silicon, which might measure only a centimetre across but can contain hundreds of millions of transistors. The transistors are joined together into circuits by tiny wires which can be more than a hundred times thinner than a human hair. These tiny circuits enable the processor to carry out calculations and other manipulations of data.

processor

microchip

chip

Processors can have different speeds, and this influences how quickly the computer can carry out its operations. Processor speeds seem to be increasing all the time. There are many different types of processor available: such as Pentium®, Celeron®, Athlon™ and PowerPC®.

Memory

An essential component of a computer is the memory which it uses to hold data currently being used by the processor. This is the **random access memory (RAM)**, the computer's working memory in which programs and data are stored so that they can be accessed very quickly by the processor. The processor stores data in RAM and retrieves data from it as it carries out its manipulations. The more RAM a computer has, the faster the computer programs will run. RAM memory is used and reused and any data held in RAM is normally lost when the computer is turned off.

random access memory (RAM)

hard disk/drive

To ensure that essential data is not lost when the computer is switched off, all personal computers have a **hard disk** (sometimes called a **hard drive**) which can store data permanently. Part of the starting-up process of a computer is to copy start-up programs and data from the hard disk into the RAM, and all important data in the RAM is copied to the hard disk during the closing-down process. I'll discuss hard disks in more detail in Subsection 2.1.3.

There are other important components needed to make a modern computer work effectively, but the ones I've mentioned will suffice to illustrate the main ICT processes involved in a computing system.

Computer software

hardware

software

The electronic components and other equipment that make up your computer system are known as **hardware**. In order to make the computer do things, such as help you to produce your TMAs, edit photographs or draw diagrams, you also need computer programs, which are called **software**.

Programming languages

programming language

A computer program is written in a **programming language** and contains the instructions that tell the computer what to do. Developers write new software using specialised programming languages. The resulting programs (or 'source code') can be converted into the low-level instructions understood by the processor. There is a wide range of programming languages to suit different types of task; if you look at advertisements for programming jobs in newspapers or online you will get an idea of which languages are being widely used. Languages such as C++, Visual Basic and Java are in demand at the time of writing (early 2005).

Computer software falls into two main categories: operating systems and applications.

Operating systems

operating system

A computer requires software just to look after itself and to manage all its components; this is called the **operating system**. The operating system handles communication with the other software on the computer and with the hardware resources of the machine, such as the processor and memory. The operating system provides a means of running the computer's application programs. It also provides a standard user interface with windows, buttons and menus so that users can interact with the computer.

You are probably using a computer with the Microsoft Windows operating system, as required by the computer specification for this course. However, other operating systems can be used with personal computers. Apple Computer Inc. developed the Apple Macintosh OS system to run on Macintosh computers. Operating systems are usually commercial products and protected by copyright, but the Linux

operating system is available free. Anyone can make improvements to Linux programs, provided they make the details of the programs available to other programmers. This is known as **open source** programming.

open source

Applications

Most people buy computers in order to run applications. There are many different examples of software application, including word processors and spreadsheet, database and graphics packages. Some are combined together in 'office' suites, such as the StarOffice applications you can find on the Open University's Online Applications disk.

Word-processing software, such as Microsoft Word, allows you to create, edit and store documents. You can produce very professional-looking documents using a word processor, with different typefaces (known as 'fonts') and incorporating graphics, such as drawings and photographs.

Spreadsheet software, such as Excel, allows you to perform calculations based on the numbers and formulae that you enter. You can keep track of a household budget on a spreadsheet, but what makes a spreadsheet a powerful tool is its modelling ability. Depending on how a spreadsheet has been set up, when new values are entered, the whole spreadsheet can be automatically updated. Spreadsheets are often used in business organisations to model financial activities.

Database software, such as Microsoft Access, stores information in a form that can be organised and searched. Databases range in size and complexity. An example of a small database might be an address book that you keep on your own computer to store the names and contact details of friends and family. There are much larger databases in use by institutions containing specific types of information, such as library catalogues, banks' records of customers' accounts, and hospital medical records.

Graphics and image editing software allows you to create and edit drawings and images. Digital photography has become very popular and image-editing software allows you to crop and resize your photos, touch-up blemishes and then print the results.

Education and training software is intended to help children and adults learn. There are a number of programs intended to teach children basic mathematics and English skills. Other examples include programs designed to train people in computer skills or to help them learn new languages.

Games represent a large sector in the computer software market. While many run on dedicated game consoles rather than PCs, some make use of the PC's computing power to achieve high-quality graphics and complex game play. In fact, technological developments for games have

resulted in improvements for personal computers. You can play games alone on your PC, but others provide multi-player environments via the internet.

Email software manages your electronic mailbox on your computer to allow you to compose, send, read and delete messages. Email applications often include tools such as a filing system for storing messages, a calendar and an address book.

Web browser software allows you to view web pages and, among other things, use the links in them to 'jump' from one page to another and from one part of a page to another. The two most popular browsers at the time of writing are Microsoft Internet Explorer and Mozilla Firefox.

There are also other applications which provide a means of sending and receiving data. For example, screen readers 'read' the accessible text aloud, while speech recognition software enables the computer to respond to the human voice.

2.1.3 Storing data

Data must be stored somewhere when it is not being manipulated. Modern ICT systems require increasingly large amounts of data to be stored for later use, and it is important that the data can be accessed quickly. Data may be stored on the computer's hard disk in the form of files.

You may want to move files from one stand-alone computer to another. In addition, you may want to move files from a device, such as a digital camera, to a computer. These activities require some form of external storage.

I'll introduce you to some different storage media in this section. However, I'll first explain the units in which we measure how much data is being stored.

Bytes of data

byte

You will recall from Study Session 1 that a binary digit, or bit, can have one of two values: either a 0 or a 1. In a computer, bits are assembled into groups of eight, and a group of eight bits is known as a **byte**. The abbreviation used for a byte is B, so 512 bytes would be written as 512 B. Although this course will use 'b' for bit and 'B' for byte, you should be aware that not everyone makes this clear distinction.

A byte of data can represent many different things in a computer. For example, a byte can represent a text character, like the letter 'a', or a number, or a space or a punctuation mark. Just to give you an idea of what this means, the phrase 'storage technology' would require 18 bytes of storage space (there are 18 characters: 17 letters and one space).

Activity 9 (self-assessment)

How many bytes would be needed to store the following phrase?

information and communication technologies

Comment

The answer is given at the end of this part.

The capacity of computer RAM is measured in bytes. A computer may, for example, have 512 megabytes of RAM. From our discussion in Study Session 1, you might expect this to be 512 million bytes. Unfortunately, things are not quite so simple. For memory and file sizes, a **megabyte** is 1 048 576 bytes, not 1 000 000 bytes! Similarly, a **kilobyte** is 1024 bytes, not 1000, and **gigabyte** means 1 073 741 824 bytes, not 1 000 000 000. These numbers are all 'powers of 2', which means 2 multiplied by itself a number of times. Probably no one would choose to define memory and file sizes in this way if they were starting over again today, but there are historical reasons why sizes were originally defined in this way.

megabyte

kilobyte

gigabyte

As Table 2 shows, an upper-case K should be used for 'kilo' when it means 1024. This is in contrast with the lower-case k you met earlier in relation to data rates, where 'kilo' meant 1000 (see Table 1 in Study Session 1). Unfortunately not everyone sticks to this rule, and there is no such distinction made for the two versions of 'mega' and 'giga'. For these prefixes upper-case M and G are always used.

Table 2 Prefixes for file and memory sizes

Prefix	In figures this is:	This is approximately:	Symbol
kilo	1024	A thousand	K
mega	1 048 576	A million	M
giga	1 073 741 824	A billion (a thousand million)	G

The golden rule is: kilo, mega and giga have the meanings in Table 2 if they refer to memory or file sizes; if they refer to data rates then kilo, mega and giga have the meanings given in Table 1.

Activity 10 (self-assessment)

If a kilobyte is 1024 bytes of data, how many bits of data does this represent?

Comment

The answer is given at the end of this part.

Different types of storage

I'll now introduce you to some different storage media and devices. As the uses for ICTs have expanded and developed, so has the need to store ever larger amounts of data. I've quoted some figures for storage capacity in this section but, given the rapid rate of development in ICT systems, some of these figures may be out of date when you read this block.

Magnetic storage

zip disk

As I mentioned earlier, your computer has a hard disk which provides a permanent storage area for your computer's programs and the files you create. When you save files to your computer's hard disk, you are using a magnetic storage medium. Data stored in magnetic form can be changed once it has been stored, so if you run out of space you can delete some files to make room or, if you want to edit a file, you can make the necessary changes and then save it again. At the time of writing, a medium-priced computer has a storage capacity of up to 100 GB. A floppy disk can store about 1.44 MB, but this type of storage has largely been replaced by new storage media with larger capacities. A **zip disk** is a high capacity form of magnetic storage which is portable. Zip disks are available in capacities of 100 MB, 240 MB and 750 MB.

Optical storage

CD-ROM

A **CD-ROM** (Compact Disk Read Only Memory) uses a laser-based optical form of storage. This type of disk has been used for many years to distribute music and computer software. A CD-ROM drive is needed to read the disks. Data is locked into the disk during manufacture, and cannot afterwards be changed.

There are two other types of CD device for computers: CD-R (CD-recordable) and CD-RW (CD-rewritable). With the right sort of CD drive in your computer, you can 'burn' data (that is, write data) to either type. Data written to a CD-R disk cannot be changed afterwards, although further data can be added. Data written to a CD-RW disk can be erased and the disk reused.

CD-ROMs can store up to 800 MB of data, 90 minutes of audio or 60 minutes of video. CD-R and CD-RW disks vary in their capacity, but typically it is in the region of 700 MB.

DVD

DVD (Digital Versatile Disk) works in a similar way to CDs, but the data is held in a more compact format. In addition, DVDs can have more than one layer of data. A single data layer can hold about 4.4 GB. At the highest quality, roughly two hours of video can be held in a layer, and with reduced quality about three hours. As with CDs, there are 'R' and 'RW' versions to which the user can write data. The 'Blu Ray' system, using a blue laser (instead of a red one), stores data even more compactly. This system promises to increase the capacity of a layer to 27 GB.

Flash memory

Flash memory is an electronic form of memory which can be used, erased and reused. A flash memory card is a small storage device used to store data such as text, pictures, sound and video. These cards are used in portable devices such as digital cameras and in small portable computers, such as Personal Digital Assistants (PDAs).

flash memory

A USB flash memory, sometimes called a 'memory stick', is a small storage device which is completely external and connects to the computer via a USB port. This portable memory comes in different capacities, e.g. 256 MB, 512 MB, 1 GB and 2 GB.

Activity 11 (self-assessment)

Are these statements about storage true or false? Mark each one with a 'T' for true or 'F' for false.

(a) The hard disk in a computer is used to store data.

(b) The storage capacity of a floppy disk is several gigabytes.

(c) Data files that you want to update regularly should be stored on CD-R optical disk.

(d) A DVD is a form of magnetic storage.

(e) A USB memory stick holds much more than a floppy disk.

Comment

The answers are given at the end of this part.

2.2 Networked computers

Now that I have introduced you to the processes carried out by a stand-alone computer, I will move on to discuss what happens when computers are linked.

2.2.1 Modelling networked computers

You met a block diagram showing a model of a communication system in Figure 8 (Study Session 1). In this model, a transmitter sends data into a network which conveys it to a receiver; but how does this model work when the transmitter and receiver are computers?

Sometimes the computer's user is communicating with another computer user, (for example when using an online 'chat' system). In that case we can consider the users and their linked computers as forming a communication system similar to that shown in Figure 8.

Sometimes, however, the computer's user is communicating with another *computer* (for example, when browsing a website). Figure 11 models that situation; the blocks are 'user', 'computer', 'network' and then another 'computer'.

To explore the model shown in Figure 11, I'll use the example of sending a message from your computer at home to a FirstClass conference (as you did in Part 1, Study Session 3).

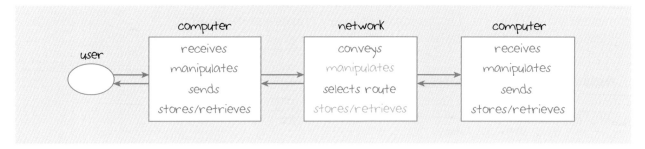

Figure 11 Computers in a network

First computer (your computer)

In the block diagram, the computer receives data from the user and sends it into the network. It will manipulate and also store and retrieve data.

If you send a message to a FirstClass conference, your computer receives the message from you as data via the keyboard. The computer manipulates the data into a form that can be sent into the network, in this case the internet via your internet service provider (ISP). Your computer will also store or retrieve relevant data, such as details of the FirstClass computer's internet address.

Network

In the same way as in the network shown in Figure 8, this network conveys the data to the receiver, selecting the most appropriate route for it to travel. In order to do this, the network may need to manipulate and store or retrieve data.

Your computer sends the FirstClass message into the internet, via your ISP connection, and the internet conveys the message to its destination, which is a computer at The Open University. The devices which make up the internet work together to select the most appropriate route for conveying the message. The internet is very complex so this will involve manipulating, retrieving and possibly storing data on the way.

Second computer (the FirstClass server)

The computer on the right of Figure 11 receives the data, manipulates it and then stores it. The computer then typically sends some kind of response back via the network, which may require the computer to retrieve some stored data.

The computer in this example is one of the Open University's FirstClass servers. A **server** is a computer whose hardware and software is dedicated to making data available to other computers. The FirstClass server receives the data from the network and stores it. It carries out the manipulations necessary to add your message to those already in the conference, retrieving other details about the conference as it does so. It also sends data back to you, showing you that your message is now in the conference.

server

2.2.2 Personal Digital Assistants

Personal Digital Assistants (PDAs) or handheld computers are small, portable computers. They each contain a small processor and have specially written operating systems. Two popular types of PDA at the time of writing (early 2005) are those running the Palm OS operating system and those using the Windows Mobile operating system, (also called Pocket PC). There is a range of applications purposely written for PDAs, but many also use special versions of popular applications like Microsoft Word, Excel and Outlook.

Personal Digital Assistants (PDAs)

Some PDAs have very small keyboards to input data, whilst others use touch screens which can be tapped with a finger or a stylus. Many can accommodate flash memory cards to increase space for data storage. Many PDAs can be used to view digital photographs or sometimes video, and can be used to play music in MP3 format. Some PDAs even have integral digital cameras.

PDAs are designed to connect with personal computers and other PDAs to transfer data between them using a range of communication links, such as Bluetooth and infrared. At the more expensive end of the range, some PDAs have built-in mobile phones and can connect to the internet to send and receive email.

Activity 12 (self-assessment)

This activity is intended to help you consolidate your learning from this study session and give you some practice in working with the technological content of an article. The article that follows (Revel, 2004) illustrates the way PDAs, an example of an ICT system, can be used in education.

You should read this article and then answer the following questions.

(a) How can a child input data to his or her own PDA?

(b) How is data conveyed between PDAs?

(c) How does the PDA output data to the child?

(d) Give an example from the article of how the PDA manipulates data.

Note: In case you're not familiar with it, the National Grid for Learning is (at the time of writing) a government initiative in the UK that provides a network of educational resources on the internet. These resources are available for use by children, parents and teachers as well as librarians and those involved in adult education.

Comment

My answers are given at the end of this part.

. . . .

MINIATURE COMPUTERS ARE ADDING UP TO FUN

PALM COMPUTERS ARE CONQUERING THE CLASSROOM, AND STUDENTS IN DUDLEY ARE AMONG THE FIRST TO TEST THE EDUCATIONAL VALUE OF THESE CLEVER GADGETS, WRITES PHIL REVELL

Phil Revell

Tuesday September 28, 2004

The Guardian

It's playtime at the Wren's Nest in Dudley. Children at the West Midlands primary school are running around, skipping, playing soccer – and exchanging music files on their personal digital assistants (PDAs).

In one corner, a couple are using Bluetooth technology to play noughts and crosses. In another, a girl is showing a boy how to change colours on the tiny screen.

The school has bought 50 Palm PDAs since February, and the Wren's Nest is in the first wave of an ambitious new project. 'We want to have handhelds for all the children in one of Dudley's townships by next year,' says John Davies from the authority's National Grid for Learning (NGfL) team.

'Then rolling out to all the schoolchildren in the borough.' Every student and teacher in Dudley? That's 40,000 handhelds.

All the kit is coming from Palm. The Wren's Nest children were equipped with the Tungsten T2, while the T3s are going to the other first-phase children.

Palm's latest device, the Zire 72, was designed with Dudley's education blueprint in mind. It features a built-in digital camera, audio/video capture and playback, and Bluetooth technology.

In phase three, Dudley's kids will be provided with a 'learner's kitbag', which will contain the handheld, a Bluetooth modem, stereo headphones and a protective case.

Headteacher at the Wren's Nest, Ruth Wylie, took a careful look at the implications before agreeing to join phase one of the project. The school serves a disadvantaged estate and props up Dudley's league tables. In the past, results have been dire. 'We are working really hard to improve standards, and I didn't want anything to distract us from that,' she says.

There was also the worry about security. Children would be allowed to take the handhelds home. What about damage, theft, the risk of bullying or even mugging? 'We've had no problems,' says Wylie. 'Quite the contrary, the kids

have really looked after their Palms. We've had accidents, but the Palms bounce pretty well. We had one in a puddle which is drying out at the moment.'

This mirrors the experience of schools involved in similar loan schemes involving laptop computers. Damage and loss has been negligible. The disadvantage of laptop schemes hasn't been the security issue, but the weight of the kit plus the replacement cost of the machine at the end of its lifespan. A PDA bypasses both of those problems.

Year 5 children at the Wren's Nest were delighted when they received their handhelds early this year. '[You should have seen their] their faces when they found out,' says Wylie. 'We had 100% attendance on the day they were handed out and attendance has since improved in year 5. There has been a huge impact.'

Children were allowed to take the devices home to charge them up, with the intention that a training session would be held in school the following day. 'But it wasn't a matter of us telling them how to use the machines – they were telling us,' says Wylie. 'They'd discovered the voice recorder, they knew the time in New York, they worked out how to change the background colour of the screen.'

One real learning plus has been the handwriting recognition – which uses a program called Graffiti. 'It requires you to start your letters at the right place and form them properly,' Wylie explains. 'We had a handwriting scheme in school, but the Palm has been much more effective.'

Children at the school are enthusiastic about the Palm Pilots. 'We can write stories, and beam messages to each other,' says Brandon Freeman. The Palm-to-Palm communication, using infrared or Bluetooth, is probably the most popular capability, but pupil Reanne Beach points out that the device has a maths programme that can be used as an aide to learning tables. 'My mum can test me at home,' she says. 'And you can use the notepad if you have to jot down your homework.'

Teachers at the school are looking forward to a time when children use the handhelds as a matter of routine. 'One of the things I would like to explore is the e-book,' says Wylie. 'Boys seem more willing to read from the Palm screen.' She is also excited about the possibilities for children to act as researchers, making a record of their findings as they go along, with pictures and voice notes.

'We make wonderful models in design and technology,' she says. 'But when the project is over, they have to be dismantled. With these, the children could make a record of what they had done.'

The Wren's Nest is not the first school to use PDAs in class. A Monmouthshire primary has been using handhelds for some time. In fact, the logic for primary heads is inescapable. A PDA costs around £200, so for the cost of a half a dozen PCs, you can kit out a whole class.

But Dudley's ambitions go beyond the classroom. The authority plans to offer the kit to every learner in the borough, child or adult. Funding will come from a mix of sources, with parents expected to pay a contribution. 'For Wren's Nest parents, that might mean the equivalent of a packet of crisps a week,' says Davies. He's trying to avoid the scenario where parents who can afford the kit enable their children to leapfrog ahead of the rest. 'We want a scheme that delivers a device to everyone,' he says.

Study Session 3: Computers and communication systems working together

The combination of communication systems and computers has produced powerful new systems not possible when these technologies are used separately. In this study session, I'll be using an ICT system in a supermarket as an example, as it is something that you have probably experienced. The material in this study session is not intended to be a comprehensive examination of how ICT systems are used in supermarkets; I'll just be focusing on some of the supermarket's activities in order to highlight the ICT processes involved.

3.1   ICT systems in a supermarket

Supermarkets make use of ICT systems for a range of purposes. In this study session, we'll look at the processes of receiving, storing, retrieving, manipulating and sending data at the checkout, and then we'll move on to the larger context of the supermarket.

3.1.1   Processes at the checkout

From the point of view of the customer and the checkout operator, a supermarket's ICT system is like the stand-alone computer you saw in Figure 10 in Study Session 2. The system map in Figure 12 represents this view. The boundary of the system has been drawn tightly, so that we can focus on the important processes being carried out at the checkout. I've called the system the 'checkout system' and there are three components: the customer, the checkout operator and the checkout terminal.

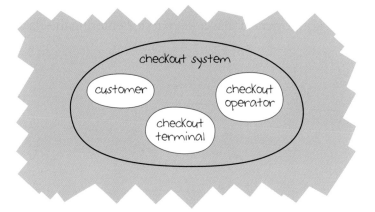

Figure 12   System map of a checkout system

I've also adapted the diagram of the stand-alone computer you saw in Figure 10 to show the checkout system as a block diagram (Figure 13). The computer is now the checkout terminal. However, there is an important difference between the two diagrams in that this computer has *two* users, the checkout operator (User 1) and the customer (User 2). The reason for this should become clearer as we discuss the processes involved at the checkout.

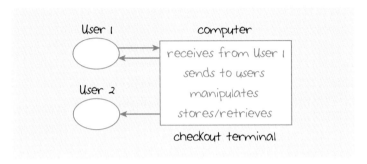

Figure 13   The checkout system

Receiving data

In a supermarket ICT system, there needs to be some way for the computer to receive information about the items a customer is buying.

Activity 13 (exploratory)

Think back to a recent visit to your local supermarket and how you made your purchases at the checkout. How did the checkout operator input information about your purchases?

Comment

This probably involved the checkout operator using a bar code reader to scan the bar code printed on the label of each of your purchases. If an item doesn't have a bar code or, if for some reason, the bar code can't be read, the checkout operator has a keypad for entering the data.

A **bar code** is a pattern of narrow and wide stripes which can be read by a machine. A bar code reader is a device which optically scans the bar code and converts the stripes into numerical data which can be automatically input to the checkout computer.

bar code

Storing and retrieving data

As each item is scanned, the checkout computer looks up its price. The running total for each customer's purchases is stored temporarily in the checkout terminal. Other data may also be stored, such as the amount of money that has been taken at that checkout during the day.

Manipulating data

Once all items have been scanned, the checkout computer manipulates the data to produce the total cost. If you are paying with cash and require change, the checkout operator will enter the amount you have tendered (an example of the computer receiving data from the user) and the computer will calculate any change required.

Sending data

As the items are scanned into the checkout computer, information about the price of each item may be shown on a small display so that the customer can see the price. Sometimes there is a beep as each item passes the bar code reader, to tell the checkout operator the item has been identified. Once all the items have been scanned, the total amount is displayed. Once the customer has paid, they are given a printed till receipt which shows all the items purchased, the price of each and total expenditure.

Activity 14 (self-assessment)

In Table 3 I have listed some of the different activities carried out at the checkout. Match each of these with one of the ICT processes associated with a stand-alone computer: receives, sends, stores, retrieves and manipulates.

I've completed the first as an example.

Table 3

	Activity	Process
1	Scanning a bar code	Receives
2	Providing a receipt	
3	Calculating total cost of items purchased	
4	Subtracting the total cost from money tendered by the customer	

Comment

My answer is given at the end of this part.

3.1.2 Networked computers in the supermarket checkout system

All these processes are very helpful for the purposes of dealing with an individual customer's purchases. However, when computers are linked in a network, many new uses are possible.

Now, I am going to draw a different system boundary. The components of this supermarket checkout system are the checkout terminal, the network and the **database server**. A database server is used to make the data in databases available to other computers on the network, and therefore to users. You met a specialised form of database server in Study Session 2: the FirstClass server which gives you access to conferences and messages. In this section, I'll focus on the network first and then look at the database server.

database server

The system map for the supermarket checkout system is shown in Figure 14. You might be wondering about the users of the system: the customer and the checkout operator. For the time being, we are focusing on the computers and network, rather than thinking about the end users, so in this system map they are not shown.

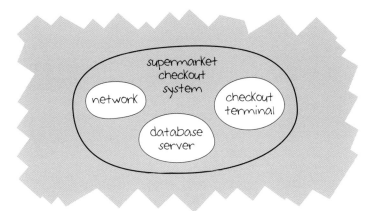

Figure 14 System map of a supermarket checkout system

The network

The term 'network' is used to describe some very different interconnected systems. In a home setting, you might have just two computers linked together to share documents and devices (such as a printer and a scanner) and to use the same internet connection. This setup is a network, albeit a small one. At the other end of the scale is a multinational company with a network of computers distributed all over the world.

A network belonging to a single organisation, where the computers are close to each other on a single site, is known as a **Local Area Network** or **LAN**. In a **Wide Area Network**, or **WAN**, the computers may be spread over a large geographic area such as a city, a country, or even across continents. The computers in a WAN are usually linked via private communication links leased by the organisation.

Local Area Network (LAN)

Wide Area Network (WAN)

When your computer is connected to a network, you have access to network resources such as shared printers and software, and to data and possibly storage space on other computers. A network can also support email and other communication services for its users.

The checkout terminals in a supermarket will almost certainly be linked to each other in a LAN within the building. There will probably also be links to other networks within the supermarket organisation. For example, there will be links to a network at the head office which may be many hundreds of miles away.

Activity 15 (exploratory)

Have another look at what you have just read about networks. Write two or three sentences to explain the advantages of networked computers.

Comment

You may have mentioned advantages such as sharing documents, devices and an internet connection in a small-scale network. In a larger network, resources such as software applications, data and printers could be shared, and access provided to an email service.

The database server

A database is used to store data in a form that can be organised and searched. A supermarket may use a number of different databases in order to carry out its activities. I'll now discuss two examples of database use: firstly, pricing and stock control and secondly, loyalty cards. I'll use these examples to illustrate how data is manipulated in a supermarket ICT system.

Pricing and stock control

A supermarket has a large database of information about its goods, such as the name, price, size and quantity held in stock.

If the price of a particular item changes, the relevant data in the supermarket's database can be easily updated. When the bar code for an item is scanned, the checkout computer searches the database for the item and retrieves the new price. Because the checkout computers are networked, they all use the same data on the database server, so it is not necessary to change prices on individual checkout computers.

Once goods have been sold in a branch, the database is updated. If, for example, you buy a box of your favourite breakfast cereal, the entry in the database for that particular item is decreased by one. When stock levels are getting low, the supermarket can quickly restock its shelves and reorder goods where necessary. The database can then be updated with the new stock levels.

Data about your purchases, and other people's, can be stored in the database and manipulated so that the supermarket knows what sort of goods people buy in that particular branch. The supermarket's management team can use this information in making decisions about which products to stock.

A loyalty card scheme

Supermarkets, and other types of retailer, use loyalty cards to encourage customers to use their particular shops. Points are awarded when a customer spends money in the shop. Supermarkets 'reward' their customers by converting loyalty card points into vouchers. They may also give them discount vouchers for a range of products.

Supermarkets use their loyalty card schemes to collect data about their customers. Data about each customer is held in a large database where each customer is identified by a unique number. This number is stored in a magnetic strip on the back of the customer's loyalty card.

When the customer presents their loyalty card at the checkout, it will be 'swiped' through a card reader to capture data from the magnetic strip. The number in the magnetic strip is read, allowing the customer to be identified. Points are added to the customer's loyalty points account once all shopping purchases have been entered into the computer.

Activity 16 (exploratory)

What personal data might the supermarket want to hold about you?

Comment

The supermarket might want to hold basic data such as your name and address so that you can receive vouchers and other promotional material. Some supermarkets also ask for other personal information such as your telephone number, mobile number and email address.

Linking data

We now have two sets of data held by the supermarket: the data about its own products and the personal data about customers. Individually, each of these two sets of information has important uses. However, when they are linked, they provide a very powerful tool for the supermarket.

The personal data from a loyalty card scheme can be used to compile targeted mailing lists, because data about your purchases can help build up a profile of how you spend your money. For example, the supermarket knows from data held about your spending patterns whether you buy products for babies, children or pets, and whether you prefer particular brands. This information allows the supermarket to send you appropriate information and special offers.

The mailing lists that supermarkets gather from loyalty card schemes may also be sold to other businesses. However, in the UK the Data Protection Act (1998) applies to the personal data gathered by loyalty card schemes, which means that customers must be asked for permission to use information about them.

Identity in an ICT system

In a supermarket we might see the following data on an item: 5018190009067. On their own, the digits do not mean very much, but these numbers are typical of the type of data input to a computer system. In this instance, they are numbers from a bar code on a jar of coffee. I have described the numbers here as 'data' because in themselves they do not really tell us anything.

When the bar code is moved past a bar code reader at a checkout counter, the checkout terminal will display details on the screen, such as these:

Café Direct coffee, 100 g

This is information which can be used by a person.

In this example, we see that the bar code 5018190009067 refers to a 100-gram jar of Café Direct coffee. We can say that the bar code identifies the jar of coffee in the supermarket's database. However, the bar code doesn't give a unique identity to the *individual* jar of coffee, only to this particular category of item.

Activity 17 (exploratory)

It would be important that any points I earned by shopping at a particular supermarket were assigned to me and not to someone else. In the supermarket loyalty card scheme, what is it that uniquely identifies a customer?

Comment

A customer could be identified by his or her name, but this is not unique as there may be many people with the same name using the supermarket's branches. Therefore, the supermarket chain needs to use a unique customer identification number, which is stored on the card and in the database.

A unique identifier is normally used for individual people and things in an ICT system. For people this is often a number, such as the Personal Identification Number (PIN) which may be used to identify individual customers in a loyalty card system. A unique identifier may also be a combination of letters and numbers, such as your Open University Personal ID.

RFID

Radio Frequency Identity (**RFID**) technology provides a means of identifying individual items. This contrasts with the bar code system, which identifies only categories of items (such as all 100-gram jars of Café Direct coffee). Each tag is unique so that each item, whether it is a razor blade or an item of clothing, can be tracked individually.

An **RFID** tag works in conjunction with a device called an RFID reader. In response to a signal from the reader, the tag transmits data to the reader using a radio link. The data could be just an identification number, which is then used to look up further data in a database. Alternatively, the tag itself could hold details such as price, colour, packaging and expiry date.

This technology has now been brought to some supermarkets. There are a number of attractions for supermarkets in using RFID technology. As the tags can be tracked by RFID readers, there is no need to scan items at the checkout. RFID technology can be used to set up 'smart shelves' that can sense when products are running low, enabling the supermarket to keep track of stock levels.

3.1.3 Taking an overview of ICT systems

I'm going to pause here to try to put together some of the ideas we have encountered so far in Part 2. I deliberately chose the example of a supermarket to illustrate some of the key processes involved in an ICT system. Figure 15 is a modified version of the block diagram for computers in a network (Study Session 2, Figure 11). I have changed the labels in order to represent the networked computers in a supermarket. I have also added the second user, as in Figure 13. I'll now take each block of the diagram in Figure 15 in turn and examine what is involved. This is a 'walkthrough' of the networked computer system and it will help us to highlight the important processes that take place in each block.

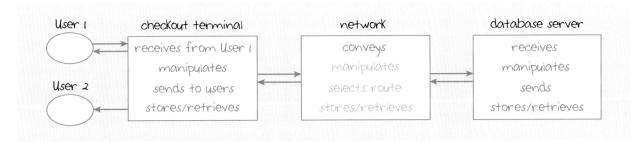

Figure 15 Block diagram of a networked computer in a supermarket

The checkout terminal

The first computer block represents the checkout terminal. The processes at the checkout (receiving, storing, retrieving, manipulating and sending data to the user), are the same as I described earlier in this study session. However, the checkout terminal also sends data via the supermarket's network.

The network

The network conveys the data on items purchased through to the database server. It also conveys data such as revised prices and special offers from the database server back to the checkout terminal. In both cases this may involve selecting an appropriate route through the network and manipulating, storing or retrieving data.

The database server

The computer block on the right represents the database server, which is dedicated to managing a database and making the data available to other computers in the network. The database server receives data via the network. It stores, retrieves and manipulates data, for example by retrieving your previous points total and adding to it the number of points you have 'earned' on this visit. This data is also sent back via the network to the checkout computer to show you the total number of points you have accumulated.

Clearly, Figure 15 shows a very simplified version of the supermarket's ICT system. For example, a supermarket is likely to have many more checkout terminals, and there will be at least one computer for use by the manager and office staff.

Figure 16 shows a block diagram of a more comprehensive ICT system for a supermarket. This may look complex, but you will see that it can be built up from the smaller systems that we have been considering. As Figure 16 shows, each of the supermarket's branches has a number of checkout terminals and at least one 'back office' computer. These computers are linked via a network to each other and to the supermarket's database server, which will probably be located in the head office.

This type of system will be replicated in each branch throughout the supermarket chain. There may also be regional warehouses with their own networked systems to supply the branches, and there will be a networked system in the head office to assist in the management of the whole supermarket chain. All these networks will be linked together.

Treating a system as being composed of different subsystems has enabled us to deal with a complex ICT system in a supermarket. Our system maps have helped us to deal with complexity by drawing the system boundary so that we can investigate a particular subsystem. In this way, we can 'look into' a specific part of a complex system.

In this study session, we started by considering a system with one checkout terminal and looked at the processes involved. We then expanded our view of the system to include one checkout networked to a database server. Lastly, we looked at a number of checkouts and the 'backroom' computers networked to the database server. As you may have gathered, we could go even further and look at all the supermarket branches, warehouses and head office networked together.

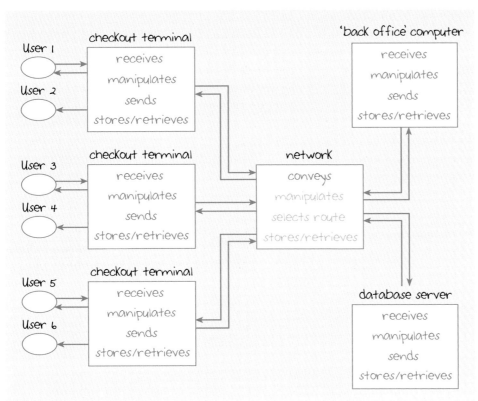

Figure 16 A block diagram representing a more comprehensive view of the supermarket ICT system

To complete this study session we will look at another way of using ICTs for shopping – electronic commerce.

3.2 Electronic Commerce

Most supermarkets now have an online ICT system which allows customers to select and purchase goods from the supermarket's website. Goods are then delivered to the customer's home. Buying and selling things using the internet is known as 'electronic commerce', often shortened to **e-commerce**.

e-commerce

Using e-commerce

Many people now have internet connections and this offers many benefits to both businesses and their customers.

From a customer's point of view, e-commerce has a number of advantages. Shopping can be done from home; you can probably find what you need without trudging from one shop to another and waiting in queues. You can also purchase goods 24 hours a day, every day.

From the point of view of a business, e-commerce also offers a number of advantages. There is a potentially wide customer base. Setting up a website and using it to do business can be more cost effective than using a conventional shop. There are fewer overheads in terms of, for example, heating, lighting and staffing. The costs of delivering goods are relatively low compared with those of running a shop. Businesses can use the Web to reach customers on a national or even international basis, rather than being confined to a shop's geographic location. The Web creates a more level playing-field in that smaller companies can compete against larger companies.

However, e-commerce works well only if the company has a good warehouse system and access to an effective distribution system. The company must have the goods in its warehouse in sufficient quantities and at the right time in order to meet its customers' orders. The company must also ensure that the goods can be conveyed to the customer as quickly as possible, which may involve using couriers and other special delivery services.

web server

In many ways, the ICT system used in an online operation is very similar to that of a conventional supermarket. There are users' computers, networks and database servers. There are also **web servers**, which are computers that hold web pages and make them available to users over the internet.

Shopping online typically involves:

- browsing an online catalogue, accessible from the organisation's web server;
- adding a product to a virtual shopping basket;
- going to a virtual checkout when you have completed your selections;
- paying for the goods using a credit card or using a special system, such as PayPal.

Activity 18 (exploratory)

What concerns might a customer have about shopping online? Try to compare online shopping with face-to-face shopping.

Comment

These are some concerns I have about online shopping. There may be security worries about using a credit or debit card in the transaction. How secure is the payment system? I might be concerned about whether the seller is genuine and reliable. I do not have an opportunity to examine the goods before I purchase them, so they might turn out to be unsuitable. I might have to arrange to be home in order to receive the goods. I might worry that the goods will not arrive on time (or not arrive at all!)

Activity 19 is intended to help you consolidate your learning for this study session. Don't worry if you find this activity a challenge. What's important is that you have a go at applying what you've learnt to a different situation.

Activity 19 (self-assessment)

Think about the way you use your own computer to get information about goods and services from the Web. For example, you may have visited a shopping website to look at their online catalogue.

(a) Figures 8, 10, and 11 each present a model of a different sort of ICT system. Which of these diagrams best models the situation where you are visiting an online shopping site? When you have decided, compare your answer with mine, which is given at the end of this part, before moving on to (b).

(b) Complete the following 'walkthrough' of an online shopping ICT system to find examples of the processes involved; imagine you are already logged onto the internet, and you start by typing in the web address of the shopping site you wish to visit:

Data is received by my computer from me, the user, when I type the web address using the keyboard. My computer manipulates the data for my request into a suitable form ...

Comment

My answer is given at the end of this part.

3.3   Conclusion

In this study session, we examined the components and processes of an ICT system that is used for an everyday activity: shopping. We started by looking at a system map of the 'checkout system' before exploring the processes involved at the checkout. We considered some examples of networks and discussed the processes involved in a networked supermarket ICT system. Finally, we looked briefly at another way in which ICT systems can be used for shopping: e-commerce.

The remainder of Block 1 Part 2 will require you to be at your computer and have access to the internet. You should now go to the T175 website and follow the links for Block 1, Part 2, Study Session 4.

ANSWERS TO SELF-ASSESSMENT ACTIVITIES

Activity 4

The first method of communication involves only voice communication. The second, the postal service, does not directly involve ICTs to deliver the message.

The means of conveying a message that directly involve ICTs are the telephone and email. The telephone system involves a telephone network and handsets. An email system involves computers and a computer network.

Activity 6

There are a billion bits per second in a gigabit per second. In figures this is 1 000 000 000.

Activity 7

(a) bandwidth

(b) radio

(c) 54 000 000 bps.

Activity 8

(a) keyboard, scanner, mouse

(b) Firewire.

Activity 9

$11 + 3 + 13 + 12$ for the letters in the words $+ 3$ for the spaces $= 42$ bytes.

Activity 10

There are 8 bits in a byte, and 'kilo' here means 1024. So a kilobyte is $1024 \times 8 = 8192$ bits.

Activity 11

(a) T

(b) F

(c) F

(d) F

(e) T

Activity 12

(a) The PDA has a digital camera for images, a voice recorder for sound, a touch screen and 'Graffiti' software which converts handwriting to text.

(b) The article mentions infrared and Bluetooth as the means by which data is 'beamed' between PDAs.

(c) The article mentions a screen and headphones.

(d) This process is a little less obvious than the others. The examples I came up with are:

- some children are playing noughts and crosses, which involves manipulation of images on the screen;

- the children incorporate pictures and text in their stories, which involves the manipulation of graphical and textual data;

- the children's handwriting is converted into text using the 'Graffiti' software;

- a maths program is mentioned;

- the children play music, which involves manipulating sound files.

Activity 14

1   Receives – the checkout terminal receives data from the bar code scanner.

2   Sends – the checkout terminal sends data to the user.

3   Manipulates – the checkout terminal manipulates the data to obtain the total cost.

4   Manipulates – the checkout terminal manipulates the data to obtain by subtraction the amount of change required.

Activity 19

(a) Figure 11 best models this situation. The computer on the left would be my PC, the network is the internet and the computer on the right is the shopping organisation's server. (The organisation's web server and database server would probably be separate computers, but for the purposes of this activity you can assume that there is a single computer which acts as both.)

(b) This is how I completed the walkthrough. Don't worry if what you've written is a bit different – what is important is that you have the same basic ideas.

> Data is received by my computer from me, the user, when I type the web address using the keyboard. My computer manipulates the data for my request into a suitable form and then sends it into the internet. Data is also sent to me, the user, by displaying the web address on my computer's screen.

The internet selects a route and conveys the data for my request to the shopping website. The devices in the internet may need to manipulate, store or retrieve data as part of this process.

The online shopping organisation's server receives my request. It then retrieves the requested data, carries out some manipulation on it and sends it into the internet.

The internet conveys this data to my computer, where it may be stored on my computer's hard disk and will be sent to me by displaying the web page on my computer screen.

REFERENCES

Revell, P. (September, 2004) *Miniature computers are adding up to fun* [online] http://education.guardian.co.uk/elearning/story/0,10577, 1314016,00.html [Accessed 3 March 2005] Guardian Newspapers Ltd.

ACKNOWLEDGEMENTS

Grateful acknowledgement is made to the following sources for permission to reproduce material within this product.

Text

Revell, P. 'Miniature computers are adding up to fun', *Guardian*, 28 September 2004. Copyright © 2004, Guardian Newspapers Limited.

Part 3
Technology news

Clem Herman

Study Session 1: Take note

Information and Communication Technologies are developing at a rapid pace. There always seems to be something new happening. In this course you'll be introduced to the underlying trends, ideas and principles as well as the applications of these technologies. However if you want to keep up with developments, it is important that you can find the very latest technology news items and that you can understand and interpret what they have to say.

In this session you'll be reading an article, which has been published in the technology section of a national newspaper. Newspaper articles are generally good sources of information on ICTs and are usually fairly easy to understand without too much specialist knowledge. You'll be given some advice on how to make the most of reading articles like this and some ideas on how to take notes and summarise what you've read. I'll also offer some suggestions for websites, which you can visit to keep up with the latest technology news.

3.1 Why take notes?

Note taking is a useful skill for academic learning as it enables you to remember the main points of an article or paper without having to read it all again. The process of summarising helps you make connections and reflect on what you have read. While you are studying you will usually be taking notes for your own use, but this is a useful skill to develop as it can be used at work or in other activities.

3.2 Guidance on note taking

When taking notes the first thing you have to consider is what the notes are going to be used for, since notes taken for one purpose may not be suitable for another.

Here are some possibilities:

- to help you understand the information;
- to help you remember the information;
- to help you explain the information to someone else;
- to highlight the points that will be useful in an assignment;
- to help you revise;
- to reveal the underlying structure and arguments.

Here are a few points you should bear in mind when writing notes:

- They should be *personal* – the notes are usually for your benefit, so they won't look like anyone else's notes. Use whatever language helps you relate to and understand the information.

- They should have a *purpose* – or may have several purposes as outlined above. When writing your notes you should be clear as to what their purpose is, and keep this in mind as you write them. If you feel you are drifting from your purpose, then you may need to make adjustments.

- They should be the *length* you want – don't feel you have to be either too concise or too detailed. The notes should fit whatever their purpose is for you. You may wish to make more detailed notes about one section and less about another, depending on what interests you.

- They should *make sense* later – there is often a temptation to jot down single words that you understand perfectly at the time but which may not mean anything to you a few months later.

- They should be readily *available* – you could make notes using Word or other word-processing software, or you may prefer to make notes on paper or in a notebook.

3.3   When is the right time to take notes?

Any time that suits you! Increasingly we live in an age where there is more information than we can possibly hope to deal with. One of the most important skills you (or any of us) can develop is how to cope with all this information. Note taking is just one skill that will help you do this. It is important to get into the habit of making notes, and the best way to do this is to find a method that suits you (and the medium you are working in).

3.4   Extra help

If you are new to studying or haven't done this kind of thing for a long time, you may want more practice at reading and note taking than is provided here. There are additional materials that have been developed for use by any OU student and you may find these helpful. They are not specific to technology, so some of the examples they use might seem unfamiliar to you. They have been intentionally developed to suit OU students of any subject area. The materials can be found via the T175 website and directly at: **http://www.open.ac.uk/learning/ study-strategies/pages/taking_notes_and_reading_to_learn.htm**

3.5   How to take notes

So what should you do when taking notes? Again you will develop your own technique, but the method I use is as follows. I read the material through once very quickly, from start to finish. I then sift through the material, writing the words or phrases I think are important. I usually do this on a word processor but you can just as easily use pen and paper. Avoid simply copying and pasting large chunks of material. It is the process of actively reading the material and putting it in your own words that makes note taking useful. Merely copying and pasting defeats the object, although you may decide to paste in short quotations.

3.6   Alternative ways to take notes

Some people prefer to take notes in a non-linear way and to be able to visualise the connections between different ideas. Spray diagrams, mind maps, spider diagrams and concept maps are all ways in which to present ideas or information in a diagram rather than as text. They are essentially the same in terms of the structure, but are used for different functions. **Mind maps** and **concept maps** are used when developing your own ideas on a subject, for example when planning a report or essay. **Spray** or **spider diagrams** summarise ideas that other people have written or spoken – in other words they are ideal for note taking.

mind maps

concept maps

spray diagrams

spider diagrams

Figure 1 shows an example of a spray diagram about note taking. The core topic is shown in the circle in the centre of the diagram. Main themes are linked by lines from the central circle. Some of these themes then have sub-themes that branch outwards. The points further from the centre are usually more detailed and specific than central topics.

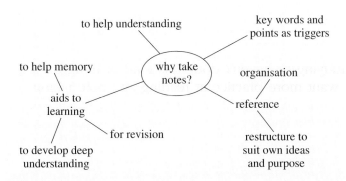

Figure 1   Spray diagram (source: adapted from Giles and Hedge (1994), p. 212)

Activity 1 (exploratory)

In this activity you will be putting into practice the above ideas on note taking. I said earlier that all note taking should have a purpose. Of course one of the purposes of this activity is for you to practise your note-taking skills, but in addition to that, the process of taking notes should help you identify what the main points of the article are and deepen your understanding of the subject matter. You should try both methods of note taking described above – making linear notes (using your computer or on paper) and creating a spray diagram (again you can use pen and paper or, if you would like to try this, a computer tool such as Microsoft Paint or the Draw tool in Word).

Below is a newspaper article written in May 2004 about a village in the Pennines which has been dubbed the broadband capital of Britain.

1 Read the article through once to get an overall idea of the content.

2 Read the article again, making notes on the key words and points from each paragraph. Don't worry about writing proper sentence; just use words or phrases that make sense to you and that you will be able to understand at a later date. You may want to use different-coloured pens if you are writing on paper, or use highlighting and underlining if you are working on a word processor.

3 Finally try creating a spray diagram. Start with a circle in the middle of the page that gives the main topic. Then add key concepts linked out from the central circle using straight lines, possibly circling the main points and linking out to as much detail as you think is useful. There are no set rules for how to do this, so you can be as creative as you like. If you've never used these kinds of diagram before, you may need to practise a few times to get the diagram into a format that makes sense to you.

MIRACLE OF THE MOOR

ONE OF THE MOST ISOLATED VILLAGES IN THE PENNINES HAS BEEN DUBBED THE BROADBAND CAPITAL OF BRITAIN. SEAN DODSON ON HOW A DRIVE FOR DIGITAL LED TO RURAL REGENERATION

Sean Dodson

Thursday May 6, 2004

The Guardian

Monday evening, Alston Moor, the north Pennines. In the gloaming of the setting sun, a broken turbine is whirring in the wind. Daniel Heery, a wiry, quietly spoken, Wirral-born project manager, is out on the moor to examine the machine. It powers the antenna connecting the tiny Cumbrian town of Alston with the neighbouring village of Garrigill and, with it down, the connection is lost and the village is denied vital access to the internet. Heery is keen to get it fixed.

Alston Moor used to be one of the remotest corners of England. In winter, just a single bus a day will take you off the moor, and the train station closed in 1974. There is no supermarket and the nearest local paper is published 20 miles away. Isolation can have its plus points, mind. When foot and mouth and BSE ravaged the English countryside, Alston was so isolated that not a single case of either was reported on the moor.

But today, Alston is a leading light in the community broadband movement. The tiny town (population 2,200) has been dubbed the broadband capital of Britain and one of the most wired places in the country. According to data published by Leeds University, Alston came second after Kensington and Chelsea with the highest rate of broadband take-up in the UK. Moreover, Alston enjoys a PC ownership rate of 88%, even higher than the internet hotspots of Sweden, Silicon Valley or South Korea.

Last week, BT announced that it is to wire the vast majority of rural exchanges by 2005. Soon, the kind of network connectivity enjoyed in Alston could be repeated across rural Britain. So what, then, does the wired countryside look like?

Back up on the moor, Heery is joined by Paul Crabtree, the local copper, who patrols the moors in his Nissan Terrano. The highest point in the Pennines is only a few miles from Alston and it can snow on the moor as late as April. PC Crabtree keeps the town informed by SMS, using the network to send out text message alerts when the roads are impassable.

Then there is Ray Cummins, the local Methodist preacher. Later this year, his church will lose the last of its four chapels on the moor and superintendent

Cummins will be reduced to renting rooms for worship. The internet helps him keep his flock together: 'it becomes a daily point of contact,' he says.

Not to be outdone, the parish council is about to begin streaming its meetings on the internet, jokingly titled I'm a Parish Councillor, Get Me Out of Here. In a nearby village, Dave Liquorice, a sound engineer, runs an amateur meteorology centre to report on weather conditions. Others use the network to share lifts to Penrith or Newcastle or to book the community minibus.

Heery came to this remote corner of Cumbria in June 1997 to help promote IT training centres in schools. He soon began to see IT and the development of the internet as a key to unlocking the town's isolation. He helped establish a pioneering scheme that would give every household in the town its own free PC. Heery then helped form a co-operative to furnish the town with a high-speed, wireless internet network. The concept of Cybermoor was born.

'We wanted some sort of democratic structure,' says Heery over lunch in the Angel pub in the centre of Alston, 'where people could have the chance to participate in managing the company and have their say. There was a dilemma that we had spent all this public money on a broadband network, but it didn't feel right to give it to a private sector company that could potentially profit from it without passing the profits back to the community. A co-operative model allows us to mutualise the public investment that has gone into Cybermoor.'

Initially, the recipients of free computers made do with a dial-up connection but, within a year, the Cybermoor project had established the wireless network offering broadband speeds. Nearly 32% of the community have now signed up for broadband, paying the co-operative £15 per month (£5 for those on benefits) and, two years later, Cybermoor enjoys the second-highest rating for PC ownership in the UK, just behind a similar scheme in Suffolk.

The cost of buying computers for practically every house in Alston and keeping the network running for three years is £1.9m, or roughly £860 per person, although the wireless network cost just £450,000, or £104 per person. The bulk of the money came from the Department for Education and Skills (DfES) with additional funds from the Department for Trade and Industry and regional development agencies.

In February, the co-operative published Cybermoor: Measuring the Benefits. It found that the project brought in an additional £300,000 to the local community every year. It also reported that 77% of the town had improved its IT skills and that 81% of single-parent families had broadband at home. The network has brought other, unexpected, benefits. The local estate agent thinks house prices have increased by 25% since the launch of Cybermoor.

Last week, BT announced it was about to convert the bulk of the remaining local exchanges left out of the broadband revolution. BT says this will enable 99.5% of local exchanges by 2005, although this still means that roughly 100,000 households will be excluded.

Moreover, a forthcoming report by the organisation for economic co-operation and development (OECD), states that the BT scheme will give the UK the highest broadband availability rates of any G7 country. The report, to be published next month, shows that no other G7 country is close to the UK's figures – the US is aiming for 2007, while France wants 95% by the end of 2005.

BT says there is still an important role for community networks such as Cybermoor. 'It will come down to customer choice,' says a spokesman. 'Many [of the community networks] only set up because no commercial company – and it is not just BT – could see a viable business case. We now think there is one as the market has moved on dramatically, thanks to the work of companies such as BT and thousands of campaigners. We would certainly be interested to hear from any of them if their services might complement our own.'

Community networks are not just confined to rural outposts such as Alston. Deptford, in south London, is about as far from the north Pennines as you can get and still be in England. The plan is to enable local council officers in Lewisham to be able to work from home or while mobile in the community. Enabling such a wireless network also hits a number of community and small business objectives, so what might suit the local council can be shared with the wider community. The roll out is expected to begin later this month, with the whole of Deptford covered by October.

'The strength of community enterprise is that it really does engage people in local communities,' explains Malcolm Corbett, manager of Community Broadband Network (CBN). 'The process of aggregation has been very successful before, not least in the case of American telephone services in the 1920s where, in rural areas, people aggregated the demand in order to get telephone services provided. It proved highly successful, and community enterprises for broadband have the same potential.'

Corbett helped found the Community Broadband Network in February last year. The scheme had the backing of Stephen Timms, the e-commerce minister, and a number of rural charities. In a little over a year, CBN has grown to include 215 community groups connected to the site's intranet. Approximately 75 have launched their own broadband networks.

Corbett sees the community broadband movement as beginning to move beyond simply campaigning for access. Now, the campaigners are beginning to organise in a way that can provide economic benefits out of the service itself. In Alston they are developing Voice over IP (VoIP) to provide the town with free telephone calls.

In Deptford, the emphasis is not just on providing a network for council workers, but also providing a high bandwidth wireless service that can be used for a range of multimedia applications, which in turn can be used for regeneration. All the artists being priced out of Shoreditch have to be able to set up studio somewhere.

'This stuff is moving very fast,' says Corbett. 'I think there is a great opportunity for communities to get involved and end up with a situation where you get not just high levels of take-up of broadband, but much more interesting uses and a completely different way in which people talk about it.'

Others seem to be moving the debate on, too. Next month, the Access to Broadband Campaign will host a conference devoted to content and services. The focus will be less on access and more on what to do now that many community networks are up and running.

'We've used public intervention to improve local conditions,' says Heery back in the pub. 'No one's going to build a dual carriageway into the middle of Alston Moor, but we've built a digital dual carriageway here and it can have the same effect.'

Comment

Here are the two sets of notes that I made on the 'Cybermoor' article. Remember there is no right way to take notes; my notes are included to provide you with an example of the differences between the two methods. You'll notice that my linear notes (bulleted list) and spray diagram (Figure 2) do not contain exactly the same information. I found that I tended to include less in the spray diagram and tried to create overall categories, whereas in the linear notes I felt inclined to include more detail. This may also have been because I created the spray diagram using MS Paint so I wanted to keep the text short and concise! I underlined certain words in the linear notes to emphasise them as key points.

Linear notes

- Wireless Network small town Cumbria – <u>Alston</u> – very isolated.
- Daniel Heery – maintenance.
- Broadband capital – 88% PC ownership – 2nd highest broadband take up (top = Kensington & Chelsea) Leeds Univ study.
- Police – SMS traffic conditions plus Methodist minister, parish councillor, meteorologist – <u>examples of users</u> developing local information services.
- Heery – came to Alston in 1997 – developed co-op called CyberMoor to set up wireless internet network for <u>community</u> as no BT service available.
- Co-op model meant local people involved. Pay £15 a month. Free PC from DfES and other grants.
- Better IT skills, economy benefits, house prices increase.
- BT has decided to extend broadband to all areas – but community networks still important. Deptford Council has wireless network – used by community groups and local businesses.

- Malcolm Corbett of community Broadband Networks – have 215 communities on website. Engages local people in community so not just about access.

- Need to develop <u>content and services</u> e.g. Voice over IP in Alston, bandwidth for multimedia artists in Deptford.

- Conference of Access to Broadband Campaign – what to do now communities have access.

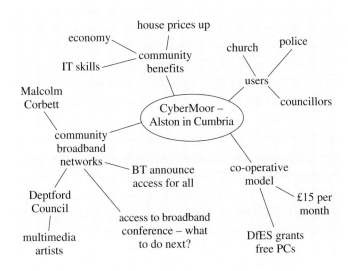

Figure 2   Spray Diagram for *Miracle of the moor*

The notes you've just made will be useful when you want to remember the main points about the article you've just read. You will need to take notes at different points in the course, sometimes about an article that you are asked to read, or at other times about the course materials themselves. Whichever method of note taking you choose, you will be developing a useful skill for further study.

3.7   Summarising

It's sometimes useful to turn your notes into a summary that can be more easily read. This might be because you want to present your thoughts to another person, or to keep a clearer record of the article or text you have just read for your own reference. Activity 2, which is optional, gives you the opportunity to practise summarising.

Activity 2 (exploratory)

Write a summary (approximately 250 words) of the Cybermoor article, based on the notes you have made. You will need to create sentences rather than bullet points and group these into a set of paragraphs.

Comment

I've written a short summary here based on the notes I made. It took a few attempts to get a final version that included all the points in my notes and still made sense. If you've not done any summarising before then it may take some time to complete your final version. Don't expect it to be as polished as the example I've given you!

Summary of Miracle of the Moor

The article is about a wireless network in a small, very remote town in Cumbria called Alston, which has been dubbed the 'broadband capital of Britain'. According to a Leeds University study, Alston has the second highest broadband take-up in the UK and 88% PC ownership.

Examples of usage include: local police who use SMS to inform people about traffic conditions; the Methodist minister; parish councillors; and meteorologists who provide local information and networking. Daniel Heery came to Alston in 1997 and set up a co-operative called Cybermoor to develop a wireless internet network for the town after realising how isolated it was. The co-operative model meant it involved local people, and with DfES and other grants, they paid for the network to be set up and for PCs in every home. Each member pays £15 a month for access. As a result IT skills have improved, the economy has boomed and house prices have risen.

BT's decision to extend broadband capability to all regions means the UK has one of the highest broadband availability rates in the world. However community wireless networks are still important: e.g. in Deptford the council network can be used by small businesses and community groups. Community enterprise engages local people in their community, according to Malcolm Corbett of Community Broadband Network who have 215 community groups on their website. Their emphasis is not just on broadband access, but also on developing content and services to benefit the local community, something that will be discussed at the Access to Broadband Campaign conference.

The remainder of Block 1, Part 3 will require you to be at your computer and have access to the internet. You should now go to the T175 website and follow links for Block 1, Part 3, Study Sessions 2, 3 and 4.

REFERENCES

Giles, K. and Hedge, N. (1994), *The Manager's Good Study Guide*, Milton Keynes, The Open University.

Dodson, S. (May, 2004) *Miracle of the moor* [online] http://www.guardian.co.uk/online/story/0,3605,1210154,00.html [Accessed 3 March 2005] Guardian Newspapers Ltd.

ACKNOWLEDGEMENTS

Grateful acknowledgement is made to the following sources for permission to reproduce material within this product.

Text

Dodson, S. 'Miracle of the Moor', *Guardian*, 6 May 2004. Copyright © 2004 Guardian Newspapers Limited.